FIGHTING THE FLORIDA SHUFFLE

INDIGORIVER
PUBLISHING

FIGHTING THE FLORIDA SHUFFLE

*The Inside Story of Corruption in the Drug
Treatment Industry and How One
Community Found the Solution*

DAVE ARONBERG
DAVID R. CAMPBELL,MD

Fighting the Florida Shuffle: The Inside Story of Corruption in the Drug Treatment Industry and How One Community Found the Solution

© 2025 by Dave Aronberg and David R. Campbell, MD

Library of Congress Control Number: 2025904109
ISBN: 978-1-964686-63-9 (paperback)   978-1-964686-48-6 (hardcover)
978-1-964686-42-4 (ebook)

Although this publication is designed to provide accurate information about the subject matter, the publisher and the author assume no responsibility for any errors, inaccuracies, omissions, or inconsistencies herein. This publication is intended as a resource, however, it is not intended as a replacement for direct and personalized professional services. Names and identifying information have been changed when necessary for confidentiality.

The images, The Florida Model in Theory and The Florida Shuffle in Practice were provided by Dave Aronberg.

Editors: Marci Carson, Linda Dessau
Cover and Interior Design: Emma Elzinga

Printed in the United States of America

First Edition

3 West Garden Street, Ste. 718
Pensacola, FL 32502
www.indigoriverpublishing.com

Ordering Information:

Quantity sales: Special discounts are available on quantity purchases by corporations, associations, and others. For details, contact the publisher at the address above.

Orders by US trade bookstores and wholesalers: Please contact the publisher at the address above.

With Indigo River Publishing, you can always expect great books, strong voices, and meaningful messages. Most importantly, you'll always find . . . *words worth reading.*

CONTENTS

FOREWORD

had a more conservative upbringing than most. Raised in a Southern Baptist family, our social and spiritual lives largely centered around church services, Bible studies, and Friday night football. That sheltered existence expanded a bit when I started playing music and came into contact with a parade of unique and talented band members who started passing through my life in high school. My parents may not have been thrilled with some of the characters that played in those bands but since my mother got her master's in music, she understood that artists often live avant-garde lifestyles.

I remained blissfully unaware of bandmates' more colorful habits, but did worry about their drug use and battles with addiction. One of my closest friends flew too close to the sun far too often and found himself in and out of rehab clinics throughout the 1990s. After struggling with addiction for years, he eventually outran the pull of alcohol and other illicit drugs that littered the music scene in the 90s. He finally seemed to be at peace with himself and proud to have conquered his demons. So

I was shaken when he showed up at my door one summer night weeping uncontrollably.

"Joe, I'm going to die. I know I'm going to die," he said through sobs. "I'm not going beat this. These fucking pills are going to kill me."

I was confused. Pills? What kind of pills? I tried assuring him that he would make it through this latest trial.

"Come on! You have been through so much worse. I know you can beat these pills. We can get through this together."

"You don't understand, man. This shit is the devil. It's going to kill me."

Six months later, my friend was dead. As he predicted, the same pills that drove him to the depths of despair that night soon destroyed his will to fight and eventually took his life.

I could never fathom how a man who had slayed so many personal dragons could be taken down by a pill. This was Pensacola, Florida after all, not a scene out of *Valley of the Dolls*. I had never even heard of OxyContin and had no idea why he proved to be so vulnerable to a prescribed medication. For months after his funeral, I grasped for answers that could help explain this tragedy. I blamed my ignorance on a sheltered background but soon learned that it was so much more. A few years later, I read how my friend's doctor was convicted of running an OxyContin pill mill that caused addiction or death for many of his patients.

Three decades later, I understand that my friend was in the first wave of victims who would be taken down by an opioid epidemic fueled by bad actors in the pharmaceutical industry, tucked inside of doctors' offices, with the drug addiction treatment complex either unable or unwilling to help him. After reading this book by Palm Beach County State Attorney Dave Aronberg and world-renowned spine surgeon Dr. Dave Campbell, I know now what I wish I had known the night my friend showed up in agony.

Aronberg and Campbell have painstakingly investigated and written this must-read exposé on an American tragedy that keeps stalking America's youth. Theirs is a clear-eyed indictment of those pharmaceutical companies, medical professionals, and treatment centers who created this crisis and got rich preying on the weakest among us through a scheme called "The Florida Shuffle."

Both authors approached the topic from their own unique perspectives.

Aronberg has made it his mission to take down criminals who used suffering patients to make a quick buck. The esteemed prosecutor continues leading the charge against this medical conspiracy fueled by well-meaning federal laws and the cravings and compulsions of desperate patients' need for relief from pain and feelings of "dope sickness."

Dr. Dave Campbell has used his unique insights as a gifted physician to uncover the medical angle of this tragic scheme. And as always, Dr. Dave has left no stone unturned. He follows the money, he names names, and he tells us how we can avoid similar tragedies like this one in the future.

As a parent, I am grateful for the two Daves' work as we all move through these challenging times. The scourge of opioid addiction, the rise of fentanyl, and the ongoing challenges of COVID have reversed decades of life expectancy gains in a few short years. To reverse that tragic trend, Americans need to be armed with the information they need on opioids, addiction, corporate greed, and the Florida Shuffle.

It is a book I wish I could have handed my friend all those years ago.

– Joe Scarborough
Morning Joe

INTRODUCTION

As an orthopedic surgeon for three decades, David Campbell, MD, knows how sick people are desperate to feel better and return to the lives they knew before injury or illness sapped their happiness. The same is true when the illness is in the brain. It is a lesson that Campbell first learned not as a surgeon, but as a brother. For twenty years, his younger brother, Jerry, struggled with addiction. As with so many others, Jerry's opioid use disorder was a tragic, chronic disease of the brain's reward centers that created obsessive and compulsive behaviors, loneliness, self-loathing, shame, and guilt. Especially during periods of withdrawal, Jerry's cravings pushed him to act without regard for the consequences.

"Chasing the dragon," known as the desperate search for the original or unattainable high, led Jerry to his final breath on a sad and lonely night in 2016. His brain stopped sending signals to do what is automatic for the rest of us and inhale oxygen. His diaphragm and secondary muscles of respiration listened to the silence. Starving for sound, they slowed, and then stopped their tightening and relaxing rhythm of human life. Fentanyl molecules gummed up the neural circuits working continuously since his first breath as a newborn, after that slap on Jerry's buttocks, his body upside down in the vice-like grip of the obstetrician in the Good Samaritan Hospital. The slap jump-started the burst of chemical-electrical signals back then. Fifty-four years after Jerry's birth, fentanyl, the potent synthetic opioid had displaced car crashes and gunshot wounds as the leading cause of death for young people in the United States. It was fentanyl that overwhelmed Jerry's God-given drive to breathe.[1]

When the grim reaper visited his kid brother, a primal instinct triggered deep within David Campbell's gut. His professional demeanor remained as grace under pressure, cultivated through decades as a surgeon, no matter the chaos around him. But deep inside, anger built over a system of healthcare that did not help his brother deal better with opioid addiction. Guilt also gnawed at the surgeon's gut, as he reflected on Jerry's obsessions, compulsions, and cravings. He knew he should have done more to help. So many times, Campbell had seen his younger brother acting like a squirrel digging for a nut: scratching, clawing, ignoring the consequences of his actions, while he continued living his own life, seemingly oblivious to his kid brother's struggles and pain. Jerry was far from alone in the United States. His death was an unnecessary tragedy of a man-made opioid epidemic built on corporate malfeasance, professional greed, regulatory failure, and political apathy.

As chief medical correspondent for the cable news show, *Morning Joe*, Campbell kept reporting on the evolving opioid crisis, from OxyContin to generic oxycodone, heroin, and the evolving crisis of illicitly manufactured fentanyl. The antidote to this epidemic, according to many politicians, was more funding for drug treatment. But that rang hollow to him in the aftermath of his brother's death, where no treatment seemed to work. Reliving everything in his mind that could have been done differently, Campbell's eyes had opened widely to flaws and fraud in the segment of the medical industry designed to help patients treat their substance use disorders.

Soon thereafter, Campbell met State Attorney Dave Aronberg, who came on *Morning Joe* each week as a guest legal analyst. Aronberg, the top prosecutor in Palm Beach County, Florida, was focused on an important part of the opioid epidemic that was receiving scant attention: corruption within the drug treatment industry itself. What if the problem was not just the poison peddled by legal drug dealers wearing white coats, egged on by corporate execs wearing pinstripe suits? What if the problem was exacerbated by the supposed solution? In a literal sense, could the cure be worse than the disease?

Aronberg's career path morphed as the opioid epidemic evolved. As a thirty-year-old Florida assistant attorney general in 2001, he became one of the very first in the country to investigate Purdue Pharma, the manufacturer of OxyContin, for its marketing practices. Elected to the State Senate a year later, Aronberg fought an uphill battle to shut down Florida's ubiquitous pain clinics that dispensed oxycodone like it was candy and tried in vain to create a state drug database to stem the tide of "doctor shopping." After leaving the Senate in 2010, Aronberg became the Florida attorney general's drug czar, a position that dealt with illicit street drugs like heroin and fentanyl, as well as diversion of prescription pain pills and other controlled substances. In that role, Aronberg helped to enact long-overdue laws (including the prescription drug monitoring database) and a crackdown on the "pill mills" that finally ended a decade of widespread human destruction in the Sunshine State. Elected as Palm Beach County's state attorney in 2012, Aronberg established a first-of-its-kind task force to target fraud and abuse in the drug treatment industry and the ubiquitous "sober homes" that had sprung up to replace many of the pill mills that had shut down.

At the time of Jerry's death, Aronberg was focused on ending the "Florida Shuffle," which refers to the insurance fraud and patient brokering schemes within the drug treatment industry that keeps patients in a never-ending cycle of relapse. During its heyday in Palm Beach County in 2016, more than 75 percent of all drug rehab patients came from out of state.[2] The most sought-after prey for rehab marketers were young people battling substance use disorder, with their parents' health insurance policies viewed as the golden ticket. Many of them entered substandard treatment facilities, lured by patient brokers who enticed them with free plane tickets and the promise of rehab in a tropical paradise. Caught in a lucrative business model that incentivized relapse over recovery, an increasing number of patients left so-called treatment centers and sober homes in ambulances or body bags.

The early foundations for fraud and abuse in the rehab industry had been constructed years ago with the enactment of federal laws that were crafted with the noblest of intentions. Ironically, it was the Affordable Care Act (ACA) of 2010, which has given millions of Americans much-needed insurance to treat substance use disorders, that provided the largest spark to ignite the Florida Shuffle in what has become a $42 billion-a-year treatment industry.[3]

The ACA ensures that drug relapse is always covered as an essential health benefit and cannot be excluded due to a preexisting condition (which includes drug addiction), and that children remain on their parents' policies until age twenty-six. Moreover, the ACA eliminated yearly and lifetime limits on drug treatment, so insurance is required to fund infinite rounds of rehab. This, combined with the throwback "fee-for-service" reimbursement model, has provided a financial incentive for rogue providers to keep patients of all ages in a cruel cycle of relapse. The more services they provide, the more money they get paid. Meanwhile, good providers who always seek sobriety grew frustrated as patients were poached away by unethical and ineffective programs with promises of free rent and other illegal gifts.[4]

Vulnerable patients hoping to recover from the powerful disease of addiction became pawns in a system that viewed those in recovery as useful only if they relapsed and used drugs again. Money flowing from health insurance companies to healthcare providers, labs, and treatment facilities became a strong motivating force for bad behavior. The urinalysis became a popular source of overutilization, as yellow turned into gold. At the peak of the Florida Shuffle, insurance companies reimbursed as much as $1,500 for a simple $10 drug test.

The opioid epidemic does not discriminate and does not relinquish its grip easily. Despite a loving, close-knit family that tried everything in their power to enable Jerry to achieve a lasting recovery, it never stuck. Even during his most strenuous work as a fisherman, or perhaps because of it, Jerry's secret stash of pills was nearby. He viewed his life matter-of-factly, one foot in front of another, one day at a time. Jerry was a kind person, even when he was drunk or high. He knew that his genetics—his grandfather and mother both were alcoholics—and his occupation in the coastal underbelly combined to trap him in an inescapable torment of drugs and alcohol. But he was benevolent. Jerry never wanted another person to go through what he had endured. He would not have wished a substance use disorder on his worst enemy. And he did not have many.

Jerry's struggles left an indelible mark on his older brother, David, who woke up every day committed to the safety of his patients. It stuck in his craw that fellow doctors had become purveyors of addiction rather than fighting the good fight against a vicious disorder of the brain. But what he vividly saw around him after Jerry's death was the antithesis of compassion, the opposite of the Hippocratic oath to do no harm. It was a continuous flow of young Americans descending upon his home community based on false promises, only to be treated like an ATM rather than a soul in desperate need of compassion.

Eventually, the many outstretched arms reached some helping hands. New laws and tougher, more innovative enforcement helped turn the tide against the unscrupulous players who infiltrated the recovery community and freed patients from the Florida Shuffle's contemptuous clutches. One community in particular, Palm Beach County, fought back and is winning. To tell the story, Dave Aronberg and David Campbell have teamed up, bringing decades of experience, to fulfill a fisherman brother's promise to encourage meaningful change and to help others avoid the same fate.

It seemed that as soon as the ink was dry on well-intended federal legislation to expand safe, affordable healthcare to those without it, some people with devious intent perverted those motives. Financial incentives in the law were misused by unscrupulous businesspeople and unethical healthcare providers, in an industry once motivated by altruism, to create a cynical churn of human lives for profit. The federal laws that enabled the Florida Shuffle still exist to entice the greedy and the heartless who seek a windfall in exploiting the misery of others.

There is reason for hope in one community's successful response to the devastation wrought by this under-the-radar tropical storm. It has, however, blown over the county lines and is engulfing other warm-weather destinations that are either unaware of the Florida Shuffle or unwilling to take on the fight.

CHAPTER 1

THE UNDERBELLY OF PARADISE

The stale air inside the sober home was tinged with the musty smell of men, mold, and mayhem. Two customers, on vacation, nestled inside the squalid, smoky living room. They had arrived promptly at their allotted time. The johns knew better than be late and lose their turn with the shackled woman behind the closed bedroom door. The pimp in charge did not tolerate tardiness. It could also jeopardize a john's confidentiality, as it meant lingering around the den of despair and making awkward conversations with others who shared the same secret. That day, the customers were dealing directly with Kenny Chatman himself, who owned the home with his wife, the mother of his small children, as part of a grand scheme to defraud health insurance companies. In this sober home, he operated a sex trafficking operation under the guise of a government-sanctioned drug recovery residence. It was a good thing for this ex-con that prying eyes of local officials were not much of an issue, as sober homes are protected under federal law from mandatory registration, licensing, or inspection.

That day was no different than most. Chatman was dressed to the nines in a dark, custom-fitted suit with precise pocket squares and a tightly cinched silk tie. Chatman projected confidence, sophistication, and more than a hint of arrogance. Behind his veneer of success and dark sunglasses, however, hid a felony rap sheet and recent memories of wearing prison orange. For someone who knew the deprivations of prison life and surely did not want to return, Chatman lived large and surprisingly close to the edge. He targeted the chained woman inside the bedroom while she was in a fragile state of recovery. That was his modus operandi because he knew her brain, and that of his other victims, craved the next high. He thought no one would believe their stories even if they mustered the courage to divulge them. At its core, the human trafficking operation was rooted in Chatman's world view that his victims were largely invisible and forgotten.

"Sasha" never thought she would end up in a place like that or need to plead with a judge to protect her from evil, but that was her destiny when she came down to Florida for drug treatment in 2013 at the age of seventeen. Two years into her recovery, she met the dapper and charming Chatman, who took a liking to the teenager, then had his men kidnap and pummel her until she lost consciousness.[5]

When a bruised and battered Sasha awoke on a strange bed, she reached for her face to comfort the pain and swelling, only to realize that her arms were shackled to her sides. She felt restraints on her ankles and tried to kick them off, but they were attached to the bed post. As she began to piece together everything that had happened, she quickly recognized she was in a bedroom of a residence that was familiar to her. This was one of Kenny

Chatman's sober homes.[6]

Sasha's memory was blurred by the drugs forced upon her. She did not know how many days she had been imprisoned, but knew she was not alone. Even though her eyes were swollen, Sasha saw other girls in the dirty living room, unresponsive from using or being drugged. This was not her first rodeo. She had seen something like this before in her years of struggling with addiction. She had just never found herself chained to a bed and used by man after man as a human receptacle. Her eyes fluttered in fear as one of Chatman's guys stuck a needle into her arm. The jolt of pain soon gave way to the soothing sensation of a sedative, and her body relaxed. Her mind wandered in and out of consciousness as a queue of cruel, sadistic men relentlessly and unapologetically raped her.[7]

Even though she was drugged and drifting, Sasha would later tell a judge: "[I] was completely aware of myself being raped, molested, emotionally, mentally, physically, sexually abused, and verbally demeaned." But there, in the moment, with Chatman in control of all her possessions, including any last remnant of self-worth, Sasha accepted that this was where she would die.[8]

Hours turned into days, and days into weeks, as a seemingly endless parade of predators sexually assaulted Sasha for a month inside Chatman's house of horrors. Reduced to a carnal commodity, Sasha relished the brief periods when she was unrestrained, only to be cleaned up of bodily fluids so she could be sold again and again.[9]

One morning, wearing only a T-shirt and temporarily freed from bondage, Sasha was able to loosen the tight grip of a window that Chatman's guys had failed to seal completely shut. She pried the window open with all the strength she could muster and slipped through the small opening. As she landed hard on the manicured grass below, Sasha began running in her bare feet across the scalding asphalt until she saw a car in the distance. Through tear-filled eyes, and with feet burning and blistering, she desperately flagged it down. To her incredible relief, the car stopped. A brave and compassionate driver took pity on the naked, bruised, and battered woman who was running through the street, waving and shouting like a crazy person.[10]

Sasha courageously reported the kidnapping, imprisonment, brutal assaults, and rape to state and federal authorities, which ultimately led to Kenny Chatman's takedown. After Chatman heard of Sasha's escape and the detailed police report that named him directly, he tracked her down using his network of fellow criminals and sex-trade customers. He confronted Sasha, forced her into a vehicle, and threatened to kill her unless she recanted the statement. Fearing for her life, Sasha allowed him to drive her to a notary to swear to a recantation of all her previous accusations against him. With haunting memories of abuse from her captivity, Sasha did as she was told. The FBI, though, had enough corroboration from others to raid Chatman's facilities and place him under arrest. His reign of terror was finally over.[11]

At Chatman's trial, the world learned that Sasha's story was unique only in the kidnapping. He had lured women from across the country into his sober homes by offering them a place to stay for free during their outpatient drug rehab. What his female residents did not realize was that the price of the free rent was their freedom. Women who lived in Chatman's sober homes were forced to have sex with strangers who threw cash at Chatman for the depraved privilege. In select cases, Chatman allowed his residents to avoid becoming victims of human trafficking by requiring them to steal purses from the tony shops on Palm Beach's Worth Avenue—the east coast equivalent to Beverly Hills' Rodeo Drive.

Facing the possibility of a life sentence if he went to trial, Chatman instead pleaded guilty and is currently serving twenty-seven-and-a-half years in federal prison. Despite the previous intimidation, Sasha mustered the courage to speak at Chatman's sentencing. "I recall close to 150 in total, different faces of rapists abusing me daily over three to four weeks," she said. "In a place where you are supposed to feel the safest, TREATMENT, I experienced some of the most gruesome acts that I can think of."[12]

Sasha explained to the court that she and her fellow captives were not allowed to leave the house without supervision. Chatman's entourage warned the young women that any attempts at escape would be met with dire consequences. Chatman went to great lengths to ensure the house was nondescript on the outside, but a fortress (and a fire trap) inside.

After pleading guilty to federal crimes stemming from his corrupt drug treatment operation, Chatman admitted to allowing drug use in his sober homes and withholding medications, food, and food stamps as a way of exerting control over residents.[13] He also admitted to running an addiction brothel, where female patients were turned into prostitutes in chains, forced to have sex with men who responded to Chatman's ads on adult websites. It was modern-day slavery hiding under the banner of drug rehab and subsidized by taxpayers and health insurance policyholders.[14]

Young men also fell prey to Kenny Chatman's abuse of the system. In Detroit, Jamie Daniels struggled with anxiety and depression in his youth, but it was a surprise to Jamie's mother, Lisa, when a doctor diagnosed her son with attention-deficit/hyperactivity disorder (ADHD) in high school. The doctor prescribed the stimulant Adderall for Jamie's condition, which became his first foray into habitual drug use. It turns out, Jamie never had ADHD. Jamie later admitted to his parents that he had faked the ADHD test to get Adderall and to receive additional time to take high school exams.[15]

As a freshman at Michigan State University, there was no shortage of individuals who tried to make a buck as underground Adderall dealers. Jamie once recounted that the most prolific Adderall supplier was an elderly woman known only as "Grandma," who comforted anxious students with a kind smile and a handful of pills. We never learned more about the woman who took advantage of the economic laws of supply and demand. Was she really a grandmother? What, or who, was the source of her supply? It was not long before a fraternity brother introduced Jamie to opioids, which was a common way to indoctrinate pledges into campus fraternity and sorority life. Jamie assumed his friend's pain pills were safe because they were prescribed by a doctor. Within five days, Jamie was hooked, and started selling his Adderall to obtain more painkillers.[16]

Two days after college graduation, Jamie finally admitted to his parents that he had a substance use disorder. At his parents' urging, Jamie checked himself into an inpatient treatment center in Michigan where he stayed for two weeks and was discharged without any further care or recommendations for outpatient therapy. A month later, Jamie relapsed.[17]

Unlike many others, Jamie had a strong support system and financial resources to help him fight his demons. His father Ken, beloved longtime Detroit Red Wings play-by-play announcer, and his mother, Lisa Daniels-Goldman, consulted a highly-regarded local therapist who recommended a residential treatment center in West Palm Beach, Florida. Ken and Lisa looked into the facility and felt comforted that Jamie would be living in a well-established rehab with strict ground rules. In April 2016, at the age of twenty-two, Jamie flew to South Florida to work on beating his addiction. After Jamie's month-long inpatient rehab ended, he moved into a reputable sober home in Delray Beach while receiving outpatient treatment elsewhere. To pay rent and living expenses, he found steady employment working for a local law firm.[18]

When Jamie first moved into that reputable sober home, an employee met him at the front door to show him around the residence. "Jamie came in the door and immediately it was very apparent that he was a very smart guy," the employee told a reporter. "He was well-educated, no dummy. Jamie, by the Grace of God, had an idea of what he yearned to do, and he was learning the process." The employee remembered that "Jamie chose to work and put his work ahead of a lot of things."[19]

As Jamie's recovery continued, he gained more hours and responsibility at the law firm. Still, the hefty $1,000/month cost of his high-quality, structured recovery residence made him vulnerable to the lure of free or reduced rent and other illicit benefits from the area's many body brokers. These smooth-talking salesmen—pejoratively known as "body snatchers"—got paid to put "a head in a bed" of the rogue sober homes that put profits over patient recovery.[20]

A manager at Jamie's outpatient treatment center lured him to a "less-intense, not as rigid" sober home that gave residents more freedom and fewer rules. The rent at the new sober home, however, was comparable to the one he was at, so Jamie responded favorably when another marketer swooped in and convinced him to move from his $1,000-a-month sober home to a nearby flophouse owned by Kenny Chatman that charged only $50 a month.[21] How can a sober home profit handsomely from $50 rent? The answer speaks to the core illegal business model of the Florida Shuffle.

The Chatman-owned sober home directed Jamie to a different outpatient treatment center, where a self-proclaimed "addiction specialist" physician prescribed him new medications, including the addictive sedative, Xanax (alprazolam), to treat anxiety. Jamie, however, was like many other addicts and had combined and abused Xanax with opioids prior to entering recovery—and now the specialist was advising him to get back on it.[22]

After Ken Daniels learned his son had been prescribed Xanax, he did some homework. He learned it is a controlled substance regulated by the Drug Enforcement Agency (DEA), as are other addictive drugs like opioids. Benzodiazepines, or "benzos," are used to treat anxiety and sleep disorders, but can cause mental health problems such as paranoid and suicidal ideation, can impair memory and degrade judgment, and can make it difficult to maintain coordination, balance and dexterity. When used in combination with alcohol or opioids, the combined sedative effects can lead to death. The Centers for Disease Control and

Prevention (CDC) guidelines advise physicians to avoid pre-scribing benzodiazepines with opioids in most circumstances.

Wednesday, December 7, 2016, started out as a festive occasion for Ken Daniels and family. For them, it was the time of year to wrap Chanukah presents and light menorahs. But those joyous thoughts came crashing down that morning, not long after Jamie moved into the seedy residence. Ken received the knock on his door that every parent fears the most. Jamie had been sober, with a durable recovery, for seven months before moving into the final sober home of his life. He had overdosed on fentanyl-laced heroin inside the very residence that was supposed to promote his sobriety. The sober home was actually a haven for drug use, patient brokering, and insurance fraud: a flophouse.[23]

"You never give [Xanax] to someone with his symptoms," Ken said. "Xanax can put you back in the state of feeling on top of the world, and prone to making bad decisions. Jamie did. He took something he shouldn't have, which unfortunately was all around him in a 'sober' home. He was found dead four days later."[24]

Adding further pain to his immeasurable grief, Ken received a text message from Jamie's last roommate seeking to extort money from the family in exchange for Jamie's personal belongings.[25] Soon after that, Ken learned that outpatient treatment centers had fraudulently charged his insurance around $60,000 for drug tests that should cost $25 each, and $1,500 for a single lab test just a few days before Jamie died.[26]

When Jamie left his reputable recovery residence for Kenny Chatman's loosely supervised, low-end accommodations that ignored drug use, it was his first, and tragically last, foray into the corrupted drug treatment system that has been known for years as the Florida Shuffle. As his anguished father would later recount: "He got coerced to move out because it was cheaper. I begged him not to go; he decided it was cheaper . . . I didn't know about patient brokering until after the fact."[27]

After Jamie's death, Ken and Lisa Daniels-Goldman established the Jamie Daniels Foundation, which seeks to end the stigma of addiction by providing the education, resources, professional guidance, and support that families need to make recovery possible.[28] The Foundation's main focus is helping children and young adults up to age twenty-four who battle substance use disorder.[29] By the summer of 2023, the Foundation had raised more than $1.8 million, allowing it to help fund prevention and recovery programs in Michigan for adolescents and young adults.[30, 31]

In an interview with the *Detroit Free Press* a year-and-a-half after Jamie's death, Ken Daniels called out the stigma of addiction that contributed to his son's demise. "Some people take opioids and don't have any problems," he said. "But for many, because of issues with their chemical receptors, they become addicted. And people view those with drug addiction differently. When someone loses a battle to cancer, you lost a valiant struggle, and rightly so. It isn't the same for drug addiction. Teens and older adults don't wish to be addicted. People don't get that." Ken explained how stigma covered Jamie in shame, which led Jamie to escape to Florida. "He didn't want people to know."[32]

Ken told another hometown paper that "it's not only what happened to my son, but many families are going through it. For these families going through this . . . we must drop the stigma of what an addict is. The family needs to put the feeling of shame aside. It's unfortunate we're all members of a club we don't want to be a part of, but there's so many that have come up to me and it's comforting to know we can be together, because this epidemic does not discriminate. It knows no socioeconomic boundaries."[33]

But most of Ken Daniels' ire is focused on the Florida Shuffle. He has shared Jamie's story to countless audiences to help spare others from the hell that his family endured. In an ESPN documentary, he relived his family's horror: "December 7, 2016, that was the day my family's life changed forever. The only nights you are at peace are those nights that you know your child is safe. My son got baited and trapped. It is one thing to have an addiction, but then when bad people get involved and contribute to it, it makes you sick. What a sick friggin' world we're living in."[34]

Tragically, Jamie Daniels' experience in South Florida drug treatment was not an outlier at the time. Facing a surge in opioid overdose deaths stemming from shady rehabs and sober homes, in July 2016, months before Jamie's death, Dave Aronberg had formed the country's first Sober Homes Task Force. Its mission was to crack down on the patient brokering, kickbacks, and insurance fraud that ravaged the once-proud industry. After more than 120 arrests, it is time to tell the story of how criminality dominated addiction treatment to such an extent that even many legitimate players felt compelled to cross the line to survive financially. Palm Beach County's experience is a warning, a lesson, and a roadmap for communities around the country who are now facing the same threats and some of the same corrupt providers driven out of the Sunshine State.

CHAPTER 2

PARADIGM SHIFT

Early one morning in the early 1890s, decades after the end of the Civil War, the palm trees were swaying with their long, flowing fronds aflutter just east of a patch of land slated to become the Breakers Hotel on the island of Palm Beach. Henry Morrison Flagler stood upon a golden sand dune covered by tall brown sea oats, blown at an angle toward the island by prevailing winds out of the east. The steady breeze carried the scent of the Atlantic Ocean and the warmth of the Gulf Stream, heated by the tropical sun in the Caribbean Sea and Gulf of Mexico.

Flagler stared out to sea without a care in the world as the wind tousled his thick white hair. Deep in thought, he stroked his moustache and rubbed his shaven chin. Already a successful businessman, Flagler was contemplating the plans he had in his mind to develop Palm Beach. Sweat drenched his back. A signature, dark-colored three-piece suit complemented his polka-dotted tie cinched under the pointed lapels of a fine, white custom-tailored dress shirt. He was oddly overdressed to be standing on the beach, by today's standards. But over one hundred years ago, that was what seemed appropriate to the oil magnate. Developing the island would not be an easy feat, but the man knew he was up for it.

Flagler had reached that time of life when nostalgia creeps into the heart. Age has a way of putting life in perspective. Experience draws attention to simple pleasures. He was nostalgic in his older years but remained a pragmatic businessman. Flagler knew he only had so many years left to live and develop his visions for Palm Beach. He was not greedy; rather he was aspirational, driven to succeed, and compelled to leave his legacy on the barrier island that was heaven on earth. Even though he was retired from Standard Oil and the Florida East Coast Railway, Flagler had the vim and vigor of a young man. He had traveled the globe, dined in the finest restaurants, and stayed in the most luxurious hotels the world had to offer. Nowhere in the world, however, left him as stricken with a sense of awe and opportunity as "The Island." Flagler was so taken by Palm Beach's beauty and business potential that he called it a "veritable paradise."[35]

Ever since Flagler first pushed his golden shovel into the island's clean white sand to begin construction on the Hotel Royal Poinciana, which opened in 1894, the contrast between the gilded life on the island of Palm Beach and the working-class life west of the intracoastal waterway has been glaringly obvious. After World War II, the disparity in wealth and resources remained on full display in Palm Beach County. The differences between the designer clothes from Worth Avenue and hand-me-downs, passed through generations of hardworking families, was marked by a bridge connecting the elite zip code in the east with the mainland to the west.

Fifty years later and thousands of miles from the manifes-
tation of Henry Flagler's dream, Dr. Arthur Sackler, a psychi-
atrist and businessman, pioneered the art of pharmaceutical
marketing in the field of infectious diseases and antibiotics. Dr.
Sackler worked for a public relations firm, the William Douglas
McAdams Company, and afterward, the pharmaceutical company Pfizer—now a giant in the industry. Arthur and his brothers,
Mortimer and Raymond (who were also psychiatrists), eventually bought a small drug company named Purdue Frederick,
which later became Purdue Pharma. Arthur Sackler's greatest
marketing success came in the promotion of Valium (diazepam)
in the 1960s, which he conducted separately from his work with
Purdue Frederick.[36]

One of his advertising campaigns for Valium urged doctors to
prescribe the drug to people without any psychiatric symptoms
whatsoever, even though Valium's manufacturer had conducted
no studies of its addictive potential. Given what later became
known about the powerful addictive nature of benzodiazepines,
or "benzos," this fast-track of Valium into the American drug
market turned out to be significant and tragic; many Americans
back then became dependent on "mother's little helper."[37] That
label became the name of an iconic Rolling Stones song in 1966,
which lamented "what a drag it is getting old." Shortly after his
death in 1987, Arthur Sackler's estate sold his interest in Purdue
Frederick to his brothers for $22.35 million.[38]

Dr. Sackler's direct-to-physician pharmaceutical marketing
strategies were employed in the explosive marketing campaign
of Purdue's long-acting, time-release oxycodone formulation,
OxyContin, onto the U.S. pain medication market. The family

business has since made billions off the sales of OxyContin, which kick-started the modern-day opioid crisis.

In 1980, sixteen years before OxyContin hit the market, the *New England Journal of Medicine (NEJM)* published a five-sentence letter to the editor from Dr. Hershel Jick and his graduate assistant, Jane Porter, that would later be misinterpreted, misunderstood, and misused to create the medical myth that opioids were safe and non-addictive. Entitled, "Addiction Rare in Patients Treated with Narcotics," the Porter and Jick letter was based on hospital records from patients with no history of addiction who were given narcotics in a monitored setting. Finding that only four out of 11,882 of these patients became addicted to these painkillers, the authors concluded that "despite widespread use of narcotic drugs in hospitals, the development of addiction is rare in medical patients with no history of addiction."[39]

The Porter and Jick letter remained largely unnoticed until Purdue Pharma pulled it from the journal's archives and used it as a foundation of misinformation to justify an aggressive marketing campaign for OxyContin. The pharmaceutical manufacturer made the Porter and Jick "study" the new gospel, even though its clinical intent was never to justify the widespread use of powerful opioid medications without concerns for addiction. Nonetheless, Porter and Jick's letter was a powerful tool used by Purdue Pharma to convince busy and usually well-meaning physicians that OxyContin was not just effective, but completely safe as well. Company representatives reproduced the letter repeatedly, frequently distributing it to physicians eager to learn about innovative ways to treat their patients. These "educational" meetings often involved steak dinners in fine restaurants and weekend trips to lavish golf resorts. In addition, Purdue Pharma paid some doctors lucrative speaking fees to spread the word about OxyContin to their peers.

As a spine surgeon, David R. Campbell, MD, who graduated from the University of Miami and trained at Jackson Memorial Hospital, experienced one of these supposed educational programs in the mid-1990s at a steakhouse in North Palm Beach. Campbell was especially interested in the topic because many of his patients complained of pain in their neck, back, arm, or leg. He vividly recalls the takeaway that OxyContin was safe and non-addictive because it did not give patients the euphoria associated with short-acting pain pills made with oxycodone.

Purdue Pharma's message was revolutionary: patients in the United States had the right to be pain-free, and opioids were the means to achieve that nirvana. Campbell had colleagues from France tell him that if you experienced back pain in their country, the doctors would tell you to sit in a warm bath and drink some red wine. But in America, the prevailing wisdom was that you no longer had to live with pain. In America, patients now had OxyContin, promoted as "the one to start with." It was a paradigm shift in the clinical practice of medicine. And like other scams and false hopes scattered throughout history, it proved too good to be true.

The Porter and Jick letter would be cited and re-cited to ostensibly demonstrate that patients who were treated with opioids had only a 1 percent chance of addiction. As in the child's game of Telephone, the correspondence took on a life of its own. Despite its brevity and lack of scientific rigor, the Porter and Jick letter evolved into what many clinicians believed to be a credible,

peer-reviewed study, in part because it was published in a leading academic publication, the *NEJM*.

Back in the 1990s, and well into the twenty-first century, if a
physician was curious enough to view the 1980 Porter and Jick
"study" with their own eyes, it was nearly impossible. The *NEJM*
did not put its full archives online until 2010. Therefore, the only
way to find the elusive and surprisingly shallow study was to dig
through old copies in an academic library.[40] For busy clinicians
treating patients with a host of painful maladies, who had time
for such endeavors? Naïveté, trust, and expediency ruled the day
then as now, although the internet has made medical research
much faster and efficient for physicians and patients alike.

By their own admission, Porter and Jick only reviewed files
of "hospitalized medical patients who were monitored consecu-
tively," not patients who complained of pain and were sent home
with opioids. Obviously, hospitalized patients under the regi-
mented care of medical professionals would rarely be allowed
to develop an addiction to powerful opioids, which made the
letter's application to the general population dubious at best.

The brief letter also noted that "there were only four cases
of reasonably well-documented addiction *in patients who had
no history of addiction.*" (Emphasis added.) But when Purdue
Pharma's minions used their polished powers of persuasion to
market doctors into prescribing OxyContin as the "one to start
with," there was no caveat to avoid patients with a history of addiction. Most prescriptions of opioid painkillers were written by
physicians who were general practitioners, not specialists in pain
management. They often did not have the training or the time
in a busy day of clinical practice to identify patients who should

avoid this new category of narcotics. Indeed, Porter and Jick's focus on patients who were less susceptible to addiction was lost on those who excitedly cited the letter as proof of its safety for all.

Dr. Hershel Jick later acknowledged that he was "mortified" that the drug companies used his letter "to spread the word that these drugs were not very addictive." He insisted that his letter only applied to patients who received opioids in the hospital for a short period of time, without any bearing on long-term outpatient use.[41]

The mea culpas from Dr. Jick and the *NEJM*—which eventually decried the fact that the letter had been cited 608 times compared to the median of eleven times for the other letters to the editor in the same issue—were too little and too late.[42] Purdue Pharma's marketing genie had been released from its bottle, with the worst yet to come.

In 1995, near the time that OxyContin hit the market, Campbell was in his fourth year of clinical practice as an orthopedic spinal surgeon. He spent many long days and nights at the local trauma hospital mending broken necks and backs, and counseling patients and their family about spinal cord injuries, paralysis, and pain. That year, Purdue Pharma partnered with the nonprofit American Pain Society to advocate that pain be treated as a fifth vital sign.[43] Clinical measurements of these vital signs are a standard part of most visits to the emergency department or physician's office. Previously, the vital signs routinely monitored by medical professionals were temperature, blood pressure, pulse, and respiratory rate. All four of these tried-and-tested vital signs share one important characteristic: they are objectively determined. As such, they cannot be easily manipulated. Adding someone's subjective assessment of pain, on the other hand, would be a far less credible clinical indicator of a patient's health, and represented a paradigm shift in the practice of medicine.

Purdue Pharma's effort to create a fifth vital sign received a huge boost when the Joint Commission on Accreditation of Healthcare Organizations (the "Joint Commission"), a respected nonprofit organization that accredits hospitals, adopted new pain treatment standards in 2001 that encouraged medical professionals to ask every patient whether they experienced pain, along with the use of pain rating scales, such as a 0–10 scale or a happy-to-sad face scale.[44] Such scales were needed, according to the Joint Commission, because "pain is considered a 'fifth' vital sign in the hospital's care of patients."[45]

At the time, it was not widely known that the year before, Purdue Pharma signed an exclusive deal with the Joint Commission to pay for pain education, including a media program with "unrestricted" grant money.[46] The arrangement led to a surge in OxyContin sales: in the year after the Joint Commission's new standards were released, sales of the drug rose 36 percent, to $1.5 billion.[47]

Safely and effectively managing a patient's pain can be like walking a tightrope. One wrong step and unpleasant things can happen. Once pain was mandated as the fifth vital sign, more nurses and patients beseeched Campbell to keep ahead of the pain of hospitalized patients. Nurses called at all hours of the night to clarify or update orders for pain medications. Physicians attempted to balance their clinical experience and understanding of the side effects of opioid pain medication with their compassion and desire to keep patients comfortable and out of pain.

The fifth vital sign eventually evolved to include a face with a frown, or a devil. To this day, some patients tell Campbell their severe pain is an eleven on a scale of 0–10. The math does not always add up, but the results are clear: when the clinical management of pain transitioned from part of high-quality medical care to a regulatory mandate, it added to the confusion and misinformation, and did more harm than good.

After surveying the carnage from the man-made opioid epidemic, one medical commentator lamented that "the misguided acceptance of pain as the fifth vital sign has been, and still is, the single biggest mistake in the history of modern medical pain management."[48] Mounting evidence of opioid abuse made the Joint Commission rethink this radical change in the way pain was viewed and assessed. By 2004, the Joint Commission dropped the designation of pain as the fifth vital sign from its accreditation standards manual.[49] Even with the Joint Commission's reversal, however, the toothpaste could not be put back in the proverbial tube. To this day, the 0–10 pain scale and the happy and sad faces live on. Although they can serve a purpose as a quick reference and a point of discussion between clinician and patient, they remain an enduring monument to the marketing power of Purdue Pharma and its accomplices.

In 2007, Purdue Pharma and three executives pleaded guilty in federal court to misleading regulators, doctors, and patients about OxyContin's risk of addiction and its potential for abuse. The company agreed to pay over $600 million in fines, and the executives agreed to pay $34.5 million and serve four hundred hours of community service, although they were spared prison.

Purdue Pharma's scrutiny may have been greater had it not shelled out big bucks since 2002 to a familiar face, Rudy Giuliani. According to the *New York Times*, one of Giuliani's missions "was the job of convincing public officials that they could trust Purdue because they could trust him."[50]

The year 2007 marked the end of the criminal case against Purdue Pharma and its executives, but the proliferation of so-called "pain clinics" that distributed opioids to a ravenous clientele was just starting to pick up steam. The unprecedented marketing campaign for a Schedule II narcotic, OxyContin, fueled the explosion of a billion-dollar pain pill industry, propelling increasing waves of opioid addiction, overdose, and death like a storm surge. These pill mills began to pop up throughout the United States, but especially in South Florida. Physicians and shady entrepreneurs teamed up to capitalize on the growing number of people with opioid use disorder. As many states tried to limit the distribution of these pills once the danger of addiction became increasingly evident, Florida's libertarian leadership went in the opposite direction. Florida said no to the regulation of pill mills, no to restrictions on ownership of pill mills, no to a prescription drug monitoring database to track and halt "doctor shopping," where patients seek pills from multiple physicians in a short period of time. Legislators also said no to limits on the amount of pain pills a physician could prescribe and even dispense. Florida was the rare jurisdiction that allowed doctors to examine, prescribe, and provide opioids all in one quick visit—no pharmacy required. Florida's Republican leaders believed that patients could be trusted to make their own healthcare decisions, and doctors rather than government were the only gatekeepers needed.

But even if a doctor tried to do the right thing, Purdue Pharma could be heard as the voice of temptation. In the early days of the opioid crisis, physicians were easy targets for questionable business tactics that played upon their egos and altruism. Although a few were lining their pockets with direct industry cash, many more were innocently and naïvely lining their stomachs with gourmet dinners at the expense of the pseudo-benevolent salesperson, all in the name of driving sales of pain pills.

The opioid epidemic was never inevitable. It was completely man-made and created in a boardroom. But while corporate malfeasance and professional greed fueled this preventable epidemic, political apathy and regulatory failure also played a critical role. Pharmaceutical industry campaign contributions distracted elected officials from the growing death toll on the ground, while government regulators entrusted with overseeing the pharmaceutical industry were largely asleep at the wheel.

A glaring example of regulatory failure came in the FDA's approval of a special label for OxyContin based on non-existent science. A prescription drug label, also known as a "package insert," can make or break a drug's profitability and acceptance by the medical community. It is one of the FDA's key tools for regulating a drug's use. Each sentence of the insert is the product of negotiations between the drug company and the FDA. To Purdue Pharma's delight, the FDA in 1995 approved OxyContin's insert that included the magical phrase, *"Delayed absorption, as provided by OxyContin tablets, is believed to reduce the abuse liability of the drug."*

The label gave Purdue Pharma a marketing coup, enabling the company to set OxyContin above all the other painkillers without such a patented time-release coating. Not only would the patient supposedly receive a smooth and steady flow of pain relief over twelve hours, but the FDA allowed Purdue Pharma to boast there was also a smaller chance of abuse because of it.

According to a Purdue Pharma spokesman, "the 'delayed absorption' sentence was added to the label at FDA's suggestion, not Purdue Pharma's, and FDA did not require Purdue to do any clinical studies to back up the delayed absorption statement."[51]

For those addicted to opioids, word traveled fast that simply removing the thin, time-release coating from the OxyContin tablets would lead to an immediate surge of super-potent oxycodone at levels previously not seen in the U.S. market. The coating was easily penetrated, as it was formulated merely for time-release, not for tamper-resistance. Soon, users were dissolving the pills in water to defeat the coating or were chewing the tablets like squirrels after the soft insides of a nut. When that proved too messy, or did not give a sufficiently prompt euphoric high, they crushed and snorted the tablets. Homemade how-to videos on defeating the time-release coating spread rapidly over the internet, helping to make OxyContin one of the most abused drugs in the history of the United States.

Not only was the reduced "abuse liability of the drug" a falsehood, but another key OxyContin selling point was untrue. A 2016 investigation by the *Los Angeles Times* found the drug wears off well before its promised twelve hours. The newspaper reported that "even before OxyContin went on the market, clinical trials showed many patients weren't getting twelve hours of relief."[52] When Purdue Pharma realized that this jeopardized the commercial success of its primary moneymaker, the company told doctors to respond to patient complaints by prescribing stronger doses, which led to increased overdoses and death.[53]

On December 9, 1996, the FDA's Center for Drug Evaluation and Research gave approval to Purdue Pharma's 80 mg OxyContin tablets. The new drug approval (NDA) represented a major escalation in the opioid's power, and a potential financial boon for Purdue Pharma, adding to its less potent 10, 20, and 40 mg tablets. Two FDA pharmacologists who signed off on the 80 mg tablet said they had "no objections to the approval of this NDA supplement, based on the submitted information . . . This intended strength is for managing pain in opioid-tolerant patients stricken with a variety of pain syndromes."[54] Notably, the NDA did not address the potential for this more potent formulation to exacerbate substance use disorder, to fuel polysubstance use, or to increase the potential for mental health disorders.

A deeper FDA dive into the potential risks for such a high-dose controlled-release formulation of oxycodone may have slowed the increase in overdose deaths. The FDA, however, never expressed concern for OxyContin's potential abuse in any of its formulation approvals. Not even in the year 2000, when the FDA allowed Purdue Pharma to introduce its 160 mg "horse pill" that should have shocked the conscience.[55]

The regulatory failure that helped fuel the opioid epidemic stems from the insidious development of close relationships between some regulators and the pharmaceutical industry they were tasked with overseeing. For example, Curtis Wright, MD, MPH, was the FDA's medical officer who led the agency's review of OxyContin, including its controversial package insert. Two years later, Wright left the FDA to work for Purdue Pharma.[56]

A leading critic of the regulator-to-industry-pipeline, Andrew Kolodny, MD, wrote in the *AMA Journal of Ethics* in August 2020 that "the FDA has never been held to account for its improper handling of the opioid crisis. But the FDA's conduct is all the more troubling in light of the close relationship between the agency officials responsible for opioid oversight and opioid manufacturers. For example, the two principal FDA reviewers who originally approved Purdue's oxycodone application both took positions at Purdue after leaving the agency."[57] In conversations with Dave Aronberg, Dr. Kolodny emphasized that over the past twenty years, every former director of the FDA's analgesic division went to work for opioid manufacturers, either directly or as consultants."[58]

Before Purdue Pharma's marketing machine, enabled by compliant federal regulators, made OxyContin the top selling narcotic painkiller in 2001, the addiction treatment industry in Palm Beach County was largely driven by altruism, with healthcare providers and facilities emphasizing safety, compassion, and quality of care.[59] As the number of people seeking treatment for substance use disorders skyrocketed, this burgeoning migration of mostly young people hooked on opioids—called "snowflakes" on South Florida's streets—helped create a paradigm shift in the industry.

Why did Palm Beach County, a beautiful and inviting destination location for those escaping the cold of winter become the prime hub for addiction treatment fraud? The bank robber Willie Sutton said it best when asked why he robbed banks and reputedly responded, "because that's where the money is."[60]

CHAPTER 3

GANGSTERS AND GREED

reed is a recurring theme in the opioid crisis and the Florida Shuffle, as it was during the pill mill era that turned Florida into America's drug dealer. Greed is the base human character trait that corrupts a benevolent medical treatment industry. Behavioral healthcare, which is the management of mental health disorders and substance use disorders, is supposed to help people recover from ailments rooted in the brain. As with many other diseases and conditions, genetic and environmental factors dictate who ultimately develops a substance use disorder from repeated exposure to addictive chemical compounds. Some people seem more susceptible than others, but no one is fully immune from developing a substance use disorder. Anyone exposed to addictive chemical compounds from drug use can succumb to a cycle of behaviors ranging from obsessions and compulsions to cravings and potential death from overdose. And it is not just opioids. Cocaine, methamphetamine, and benzodiazepines are addictive. For a brief time, Flakka (the "zombie drug") was popular in the illicit drug industry. Flakka is a synthetic stimulant known to cause violent, dangerous acts in its users. In recent years, the powerful opioid, fentanyl, has been causing huge numbers of overdose and death.

Individuals with changes to the neural pathways in the brain are at increased risk for exploitation. Add to that new federal benefits and mandated insurance reimbursements, and you have the embers for a fire of mass corruption. Moreover, there is no universal standard of care for those with substance use disorder, which allows anyone to market the potential efficacy of their revolutionary new treatment program. The complex condition of substance use disorder makes easy prey for predators searching to make a buck, regardless of the human carnage.

Effectively treating those who battle addiction is a complex balance that requires a comprehensive, multifaceted approach. Some programs demand total sobriety, while others lean heavily on medications that diminish cravings and other symptoms of withdrawal. Behavior therapy to help the recovering individual develop and maintain coping skills is often an important part of treatment. A growing body of evidence has shown that longer-term, yet less-intensive therapy is more effective than short bursts of acute treatment. Unscrupulous players in the drug treatment industry, however, put profit over people, exploiting the vulnerable and defrauding health insurance companies who pay for testing and treatment. These greedy individuals see profit in perpetual relapse rather than an enduring recovery. For them, sobriety does not pay.

The disease of addiction creates such intense cravings that, when a person in recovery is offered a chance to take drugs again by a rogue marketer or supposed friend, the behaviors needed to resist the exploitation—such as the understanding of consequences—are easily overcome. Society casts a long shadow of stigma over people who use and develop addiction to opioids. Prejudice and bias create the mistaken belief that drug addiction is a sign of a character flaw. Greed is a character flaw. Arrogance, selfishness, and hate are character flaws. It is chemical exposure, not a deficit of morals or ethics that leads to substance use disorder. It is the changes within the neural circuits of the brain that create and maintain addiction. This is not the case for the entrepreneurs who created and perpetuated the Florida Shuffle. They are the ones motivated by a moral failing. They are the ones who willingly allow greed to blind them to the harm caused by enticing a young person in the fragile state of recovery to use drugs again.

The federal government's Substance Abuse and Mental Health Services Administration (SAMHSA) has acknowledged that opioid use disorder is a brain disease.[61] It is a long-term illness that cannot be cured with short-term, intensive outpatient treatment (IOP). "You cannot say, 'Hey, you're cured, go home,'" said Alan Johnson, chief assistant state attorney for Palm Beach County. "But after the five weeks of therapy are up, the brokers and marketers say, 'here's $50. Go get a cup of coffee. When you test positive, we'll put you back into rehab.' That is the Florida Shuffle." For the brokers and marketers working the system, a patient with health insurance that pays top dollar for services is a gold mine to fight over.[62]

In a nutshell, the Florida Shuffle describes the recruitment of drug users with good health insurance to repeatedly enter treatment and live in sober homes, which allow the facilities to exploit the patients for profit without any concern for their medical needs. The victim, even when complicit in the transaction, like accepting free or reduced rent in a sober home, a carton of cigarettes, or money to buy more drugs, is not directly to blame. Rarely, if ever, is the victim charged with healthcare fraud. The predator is the businessperson, marketer, doctor, nurse practitioner, physician's assistant, or lab technician who sets out to make a profit on the brain disease of addiction.

Johnson said of one young woman who shuffled through multiple corrupted players, facilities, and sober homes in the system: "All this stuff pays. Sobriety, you go home. You're free of the cycle of addiction. But that's not what these nefarious characters are after. They want big profit on the backs of recycling patients. This young lady was brought down for treatment and was only here for seven months when she died of an overdose. The questionable providers billed the insurance company over $600,000." Johnson emphasized that she was only one example of hundreds who met that same fate.[63]

In that particular case, the urinalysis labs would charge insurance $4,000 to $5,000 per test and end up getting paid between $1,500 and $2,000 each time. As with many of these victims, she went to IOP three times per week for three hours per day. Each time she went to treatment, the facility would immediately take the urinalysis and dutifully send it to the lab. Both sides, the testers and the treaters, made thousands of dollars for the "yellow gold," as they called it. And the tests were not just for illegal drugs. "They would test people for nicotine and caffeine," Johnson said, "even though they knew the patients drank coffee and smoked cigarettes. It was the wild, wild west here in Palm Beach County."[64]

Addiction treatment began as a vibrant, caring, and effective industry in Palm Beach County. "Back then, many sober homes were mom and pop facilities run by a husband and wife," said Chief Investigator Ted Padich, of Palm Beach County's Sober Homes Task Force. "Perhaps one or both were recovering from addiction, perhaps in long-term recovery." He found that many were just trying to give back to the system and help other people in recovery.[65]

In late 2013 and early 2014, addiction treatment facilities and sober homes morphed into something different. Something darker and more sinister. "It was during that time," Padich said, "when, in my opinion, people who had no business being in the recovery industry realized they could make a lot of money very fast by billing insurance companies. And the supposed 'treatment' became more about money reimbursed from insurance carriers than the care for the patient."[66]

It became increasingly evident that providers were gaming the system. When an out-of-state patient came to Florida, the testing and treatment were billed as out-of-network charges, which maximized the reimbursement. The in-network providers were back up north, or out west, or anywhere but in South Florida. "Out-of-network means 'more dollars,'" Johnson said. "You can charge whatever you want to charge, and the insurance companies are required to pay a reasonable amount of money." In addition, the short-term, intensive treatment framework—which remains the most common treatment model to this day—was doomed to fail. "The patients would go through a short period, a burst of treatment, which is not effective for opioid addiction," said Johnson. That didn't matter for the patient brokers and marketers motivated by insurance largesse.[67]

During the Florida Shuffle's heyday in Palm Beach County, brokers and marketers cozied up to addicted individuals and their families, offering all manner of illegal enticements such as free one-way flights to Florida and free or sharply discounted housing. After patients were securely housed in a detox center, inpatient facility, or sober home, brokers and marketers cultivated their prey, preparing for when the individual would eventually graduate from addiction treatment. Once on their own with a fragile sobriety and health insurance benefits that were exhausted, the recent graduates were extremely vulnerable to the predators bearing cash or drugs or both to go on a bender in a nearby motel. The goal was to make the recovering addict "pee dirty" and become eligible for yet another round in the Florida Shuffle, paid for by insurance, as required by federal law. For young people battling the scourge of substance use disorder, the alternative was often worse: leave South Florida to return home to the troubled streets of their former life, live with their judgmental, overbearing parents, and find a job. Or they could feed the cravings of their damaged brains, party like a depraved rock star, and then begin the cycle anew.

It is hard enough for individuals with substance use disorder to remain sober when temptation lurks around every corner, let alone to remain sober knowing their abstinence will cost them their free housing, their local friends in the rehab community, and their illicit benefits like free cigarettes and motorized scooters. Because of perverse incentives unwittingly set up by well-intended federal laws, the path of least resistance, then in Palm

Beach County and now across the country, is to submit to the Florida Shuffle.

"Michael" lived that reality. "My biological mother and father are both addicts," he began. "While I don't know my biological father, I did meet my biological mom later in life."[68]

Michael's mother was addicted to heroin and gave him up for adoption at birth. He did not say what substance use disorder his father had. As a child of parents with severe substance use disorders, Michael was one of the fortunate ones. A wonderful, caring Christian family in California adopted him. He laughed, as he still calls them "goody goodies." They raised him in a strict religious household where alcohol was rare and no one smoked cigarettes—except for Michael.

He took up cigarette smoking sometime between eight and ten years old. While his friends were playing Little League, or had joined the Cub Scouts, Michael was smoking a pack a day. Incredibly, his mother—who was a nonsmoker and strict in all other areas of upbringing—bought his cigarettes. To this day, Michael cannot imagine what she was thinking.[69]

By the time he was fifteen, Michael was using a variety of illicit drugs. On his birthday, he inexplicably decided to give himself a gift and graduate to heroin and methamphetamines. Life went off the rails from there.

Only a few years later, Michael met "Anita" in a shady sober living home in Palm Beach County after they had both completed brief stints in inpatient rehab. Except the home wasn't really sober, as drug and alcohol use were rampant. And it was co-ed, which generally increases the risk for relapse. Michael and Anita proved that point.[70]

"That sober home was run by a dude who had previous arrests for patient brokering," Michael said. He and Anita remained a couple after leaving the residence and moved back west to make a fresh start. Michael's sobriety, however, was short-lived. He relapsed and attempted detox and inpatient treatment back in Florida again, assisted by a patient broker who gave him and Anita free, one-way plane tickets to West Palm Beach. Since one or both of them had health insurance at the time, the broker stood to profit handsomely by keeping the couple together. Michael insists that he did not know back then that the airfare gifts were illegal. "Neither did my parents," he added. "God bless them."[71]

After completing a thirty-day inpatient program, Michael moved to a sober home in Palm Beach County. Anita stood by his side throughout her boyfriend's short-lived recovery process, while she continued to use drugs. "It was probably the most legitimate sober home I lived in," he said. Michael credits the operators with teaching residents how to pay bills and conducting drug tests with a zero-tolerance policy for relapses. Unfortunately for Michael, the high-quality sober home kicked him out a few months later after testing positive for marijuana, although he still maintains it was a false positive result. His problems compounded when his parents did not allow him to return home, insisting he remain in a sober home, or at least not return to his parents' home until he had proven that he was in a stable recovery. That was about the time Michael and Anita became associated with a prominent marketer in the drug treatment industry, whom he calls "The Man."[72] By then, with the negative influence of Anita's continued drug use, Michael had relapsed.

For quite a few years after first meeting The Man, Michael

and Anita were still a couple, cycling through at least thirty rehabs and sober homes. Michael told us that he and Anita had no
intention of "getting clean." They told The Man the same thing, as
sobriety was not part of their life plan. In turn, The Man would
accommodate their wishes, sending them to various drug treatment centers and shady sober homes that would process dirty
urinalyses. That was as long as Michael or Anita continued to
have health insurance coverage with generous benefits.[73] The
financial motivation for The Man was profound. The obsessions,
compulsions, and cravings of addiction for the couple were even
more compelling and sad.

"I was hired by the house," Michael said. As willing participants in this insurance scheme, Michael and Anita would start
in a partial hospitalization program (PHP), where they would
attend group meetings and live on the premises. While the circumstances varied over time, they were almost always treated as
a couple. After a few days of PHP, they would move to an IOP
and reside in a shady sober home off-site. Moving to the IOP
meant it was time to get a job and start paying rent.[74]

The key to enrichment, the gravy train, was the marketer.
"The Man chose your rehab," Michael said. "He would even drive
me and Anita to the facility and offer us a free carton or two of
cigarettes."[75]

After one or both of them completed two weeks of inpatient
treatment, The Man would pick them up and give them cash,
typically about $1,500. He would then offer to drop Michael and
Anita off wherever they wanted to live temporarily. It was a lucrative, never-ending cycle for the treatment facilities, sober homes,
The Man—and the couple. As long as they remained enrolled in

a health insurance plan, they were entitled to another round of inpatient and outpatient care after the inevitable relapse. When a round of care ended, The Man would usually transport them to a cheap motel for a three-day drug bender. Once the drugs and money ran out, Michael or Anita would find a phone and request a pickup by The Man. A quick trip to a clinic to provide a urine sample full of illicit drug metabolites would be the key to another stint in inpatient drug rehab.

The healthcare providers were complicit in the process, sometimes passively, by turning a blind eye to the cycle of the Florida Shuffle, or at other times, taking an active role in the corruption of the healthcare system. Being squeaky clean was not a requirement for this brand of medical practice. The providers and patients were entangled in a web of lies and deceit. For those who were part of this scheme, payment for even unethical healthcare services was the obvious motivation. For patients, the brain disease of addiction kept them coming back for more, in a tragic and seemingly endless cycle.

For Michael and Anita, their health insurance continued to pay for unlimited cycles of what was generally a two-week inpatient rehab. That was, as long as they continued to "test dirty." It was another pejorative term used by Michael, and many people we have spoken with, to describe a urine sample found to have chemical evidence of illicit or unprescribed drugs.[76] Terms like addict, junkie, and test dirty, while still in common use, only serve to perpetuate stigma and bias.

While in treatment, Michael and Anita would be placed on Suboxone to counteract the agonizing withdrawal symptoms. It made the weeks of inpatient drug rehabilitation a relatively painless experience. As soon as the rehabs discharged them, Michael and Anita would rush to get high. Drug binge after drug binge, Mike and Anita went back and forth to the same fleabag motel, with the U.S. healthcare system subsidizing their actions. This cycle lasted about two-and-a-half years until Anita's death from an overdose.[77]

"I've taken every drug under the sun," Michael admitted. "I even did Flakka while I was in Florida. At the end of the day, I chose my path in life, and I've dealt with the consequences. I made my peace with my maker. If it wasn't for losing Anita, I'd still be using drugs. I'd probably still be in the Florida Shuffle with her if she were still alive today."[78]

Michael described his final inpatient treatment center as "like staying in a jail cell," with the beds and food trays seemingly re-purposed from an old psychiatric hospital. But that level of aus-terity was what he needed. He credits his long-term recovery to the lack of frills and harsh reality that the facility offered. Michael explains that he has remained "clean because of that place. It was a hole but just what I needed to straighten out my life."[79]

That final drug rehab experience was in a public facility op-erated by the State of Florida. After Anita's death, Michael was able to secure one of the few public beds still in existence in an industry largely privatized and entirely decentralized. Although state-run programs are generally no frills, they are largely im-mune from the dirty money and perverse incentives that have infected some in the private drug rehabilitation industry.[80]

"I'm very, very blessed to be where I'm at today," Michael said. "Heroin addiction has really put me through the ringer. My boss knows my story, which has been very comforting. He gave me a chance and pays me decently. My family is back in my life, and my parents are super-supportive."[81]

Michael successfully combined the best of two different addiction treatment philosophies: the resilience-building components of a twelve-step program with an evidence-based addiction treatment program using medication-assisted treatment (MAT) and counseling. He used these physiological, spiritual, and pharmacological tools to mitigate the cravings and compulsions of addiction while managing his recovery. Although this combination therapy is not universally recommended, and at times these tools conflict with each other, it worked for him.[82]

Michael learned fast that abstinence programs can be helpful for those with alcohol use disorder, but they are less compatible with the harsh reality of an opioid addiction. MAT uses evidence-based drug therapy combined with cognitive-behavioral therapy for a better chance of achieving durable, long-lasting recovery, and is recognized by most in the scientific and medical community, along with state and federal regulatory agencies.[83]

Michael did not quit everything, as is often the case for those in recovery. He still smokes cigarettes and says that quitting heroin was hard, but tobacco has been the hardest thing to stop.

Beneath the tough veneer of a "heroin addict" in recovery, Michael was a hopeless romantic. He had a soft spot in his heart for Anita, even years after her death. Now with children of his own, he is a family man with a renewed purpose in life.

"I loved that girl. I absolutely will always unconditionally love that girl," he mused wistfully. Then he added, with a sense of fateful realization: "There is one thing that me and Anita were really good at. It was getting high."[84]

CHAPTER 4

DO NO HARM

When the big boss calls you into his office, it is always a major deal. In 2001, Florida Attorney General Bob Butterworth handed his newly minted assistant attorney general a magazine article about a new drug, OxyContin, that was leading to massive addiction and premature death in Appalachia. Butterworth did not want this to happen in the Sunshine State and wanted someone to investigate it. That is how coauthor Dave Aronberg became one of the first in the country to investigate Purdue Pharma for its marketing misdeeds.

Aronberg was stunned to find such aggressive marketing directed at patients themselves. When it came to the marketing campaigns Purdue developed for selling their Schedule II narcotic, there was no historical precedent. Branded swag included OxyContin fishing hats, pedometers, stuffed animals, Swiss Army knives, and coffee mugs. Knowing that America's geriatric population was particularly susceptible to pitches of a pain-free life with no consequences, Purdue Pharma targeted seniors with a swing music CD. Entitled "Swing is Alive," the CD's cover showed a happy elderly couple dancing to the sounds from their youth. At the bottom of the CD cover were the words, "Swing in the right direction with OxyContin."

For Aronberg, OxyContin's branded coffee mugs were particularly galling. Although Purdue Pharma representatives told Aronberg back in 2001 that their drug was not marketed to first-time users with basic soreness, the company's own marketing campaign exposed this lie: on the back of the freebie coffee mugs they gave out to the public were the words: "The one to start with."

To this day, Aronberg regrets the lost opportunity to curtail OxyContin's growth in the early 2000s. When Purdue Pharma learned that the Florida Attorney General's office had started the first state investigation into its marketing practices, the company hired a lobbyist who had run Attorney General Butterworth's first successful political campaign and had served as his chief of staff.

The Purdue Pharma lobbyist acknowledged the rising number of individuals addicted to OxyContin by breaching the time-release coating through crushing the pills or dissolving them in liquid. The lobbyist, however, denied the company's responsibility. To Aronberg's relief, Attorney General Butterworth, known for his integrity and soft-spoken leadership, insisted that the investigation continue regardless of any political pressure.

But in 2002, Aronberg was elected to the Florida Senate, which required him to leave the AG's office. When then-Senator Aronberg was no longer part of the AG's office, another assistant attorney general took over the investigation. Since this was a civil investigation, the company was never charged with a crime. Instead, the AG's office would get companies like this to enter into an Assurance of Voluntary Compliance that would essentially be a settlement contract to change their ways and pay a penalty. Soon after Aronberg's departure, the office reached a settlement with Purdue Pharma that required the company to pay Florida millions of dollars to establish a much-needed pre-scription drug monitoring program (PDMP) to reduce the over-utilization of prescription pain pills and put a lid on the practice of doctor shopping. Among other things, Purdue Pharma also agreed to change its egregious marketing practices and pulled its most potent and dangerous 160 mg product from the market, which Aronberg pejoratively called a "horse pill"—unfit for hu-man consumption.

Unfortunately, most of the Purdue Pharma settlement money expired when the Florida legislature repeatedly blocked implementation of the PDMP because of concerns over patient privacy and "big government." One of the nation's first investiga-tions into Purdue Pharma started with great promise yet ended with an unsatisfying settlement that would be gutted even fur-ther by an ignorant legislature, paving the way for a decade of destruction.[85]

Florida's refusal to take early and aggressive action to stem the growing opioid crisis had devastating consequences. By the early 2000s, people addicted to opioids and those willing to cross state lines to traffic in illicit prescription pain pills flocked to Florida's deregulated pain clinics. These fly-by-night "health care" facili-ties dispensed OxyContin and generic short-acting oxycodone with almost unrestricted access. Long lines outside these pill mills became the norm, with license plates from midwestern and Appalachian states donning the stream of cars with desperate drivers trying to enter the crowded strip malls that housed these drug-dealing clinics. By 2010, there were more pain clinics than McDonald's restaurants in Florida.[86]

That same year, Campbell was visiting a family member who lived less than a block from his home when a car packed with six young adults from Florida's panhandle (hundreds of miles away) drove up to the house. The scraggly, tough-looking crew were on their way to a "doctor's office," where they were to receive an allotment of pain medication. Campbell's family member apologized to him after the car left, explaining that one of the young men was a cousin who had stopped just to say hello—a vivid representation of the lure of the pill mill industry on full display. In just the first half of 2010, Florida doctors dispensed more than 41.3 million oxycodone pills—compared to 4.8 million pills that doctors dispensed in every other state combined! Meanwhile, Purdue Pharma raked in $31 billion in revenue.[87]

A month later, Campbell was on the back porch of his home just north of Jupiter, Florida, reading a surgical journal when he received a phone call from a law enforcement officer. He was not alarmed, because his father had been the chief of police of his bucolic hometown of Greenacres City, Florida. Growing up in the central region of Palm Beach County was like being in Mayberry R.F.D. Speaking with police officers was always a part of his life. Still, the call seemed odd. The officer told Campbell that one of his patients had survived an overdose of pain medication. The family reportedly had found a pain pill bottle at the bedside with "David R. Campbell, MD" as the prescribing doctor. Campbell recognized the patient's name as someone he had operated on a few years before. Because she had recovered uneventfully from the surgical procedure, he had not seen her as a patient since then. His antenna went up and wondered: *How could this happen? Is someone using my DEA number without my knowledge? Did one of my employees or colleagues prescribe pain medications for my former patient?*

While they were talking on the phone, and with a million terrible possibilities ping-ponging in Campbell's head, the police officer further inspected the pill bottle, which he said was well-worn and smudged. The prescribing date was three years prior, right around the date of the patient's spinal surgery. The next day in the hospital, a detective for the police department questioned the overdose survivor and learned that the empty pill bottle was used to store illicit pain pills purchased from a local drug dealer. The pill bottle was a decoy. It was used to hide the patient's stash in plain sight from inquisitive family members.

For most of his colleagues, such a call would have been a shock. Medical school does not offer classes on responding to police interrogations, but investigations into the proliferation of prescription drug diversions was a sign of the times. From Campbell's days as a medical student through his early years as a practicing surgeon in the early '90s, opioid pain medications were used mainly for trauma, a major operation, cancer, end-of-life, and palliative care. Doctors relied on fentanyl in combination with other anesthetic agents during surgery. Before the launch of OxyContin in the mid-'90s, most of the prescriptions Campbell wrote for post-surgery pain and musculoskeletal injury were limited to thirty pills, and rarely up to sixty pills.

One of his orthopedic surgery professors, Dr. Mark Brown, was especially cautious with opioid pain medication in his spinal surgery patients. In retrospect, Brown was prescient. He routinely prescribed just a small number of mild prescription pain pills. In the mid- and late 1980s, even after major lumbar spinal surgery, patients of Brown did just fine with one or two dozen pills to relieve the post-operative pain. Back then, most of Campbell's fellow orthopedic surgery residents at Miami's Jackson Memorial Hospital thought Brown was too stingy with pain medication. *Boy, how right he was.* The surgical community has now come around to Brown's approach. The best practice is to supply patients with the least powerful pain medication, in the smallest number and dosage, needed to control their pain.

Physicians, then and now, search for better methods to safely treat the unpleasant sensation of pain, and the vast majority practice within standards of professionalism and in compliance with applicable laws. Society holds them to the professional standard of Hippocrates, a father of modern medicine, to first do no harm. During the heyday of OxyContin and the proliferation of pill mills, however, too many doctors became enthralled by the booming business of pain relief—especially those without specialized training. One study found that among doctors charged with criminal or administrative offenses relating to opioid prescribing, 39.3 percent were general practitioners compared to 3.5 percent who were pain specialists.[88] The lure of thousands of dollars a day in cash just to write opioid prescriptions to anyone and everyone who walked through the door turned some, in one of the world's most respected professions, into legal drug dealers in white lab coats.

Finally, in 2011, Florida lawmakers shut down the pill mill industry. But the damage was irreversible. Florida had already supplied the country with enough pain pills to create a seemingly bottomless pool of opioid-addicted Americans. Even after Florida cracked down on the supply of these addictive drugs, the demand did not go away. Instead, the yearning for opioids moved to a cheaper and more accessible substitute: heroin.

The modern-day reality of heroin is that users can sniff or smoke it before transitioning, inevitably, to injection.[89] Today's heroin is inexpensive, easy to administer, and much more potent than the heroin of yesteryear. Heroin dealers can increase their profits by spiking it with a slight portion of synthetic fentanyl. Illicitly manufactured fentanyl is fifty times more powerful than heroin and one hundred times more potent than morphine. It is much cheaper to produce because it is completely synthetic, made in a lab, rather than derived from a poppy plant.

These chemically manufactured drugs had largely been shipped through the U.S. Postal Service directly into the United States from China until the full implementation of the Synthetics Trafficking and Overdose Prevention (STOP) Act of 2018. The law required all senders of international mail packages to provide shipping information to U.S. Customs and Border Protection, including the names and addresses of the shipper and recipient.[90] In response to this, and some increased scrutiny by the Chinese government, Chinese drug manufacturers have shifted to shipping precursor chemicals that can be synthesized into fentanyl by Mexican drug cartels and then driven across the U.S. southern border.[91]

Drug users, and even many drug dealers, do not even know

whether their heroin has been spiked with fentanyl, since it may be added to the supply higher in the distribution chain.[92] When fentanyl or its more powerful cousin, carfentanil, are present, the reversal agent of Narcan (naloxone) requires multiple doses in a desperate attempt to save someone's life.[93], [94] Carfentanil is used by veterinarians to sedate large animals like elephants!

Because of its potency, prevalence, and price, the opioid crisis has become a fentanyl crisis. The latest data in Palm Beach County show that fentanyl and its analogs were present in 92 percent of all opioid overdose deaths in 2023.[95] A saltshaker filled with fentanyl could contain tens of thousands of lethal doses.

Physicians have long known of the potential for diversion of pharmaceutical-grade fentanyl. It is locked up tight in the anesthesia and pharmacy workrooms, and a rigorous system of controls is designed to prevent diversion, which is a euphemism for theft. Every system, however, is only as effective as the people who manage it. Back in the 1980s, when Campbell started his surgical training, it was not unusual for anesthesiology residents to walk in and out of the operating room sporting a small syringe of fentanyl or morphine in the top pocket of their surgical scrubs. Pharmaceutical-grade fentanyl was universally administered as an anesthetic agent. In the 1960s, after FDA licensing, Sublimaze (fentanyl), quickly became the choice for intravenous anesthesia in the operating room, and other potent analogs like sufentanil, alfentanil, lofentanil, and remifentanil soon followed. For any medical professional struggling with an opioid use disorder, the widespread availability in hospitals was a recipe for disaster.

During his surgical training, Campbell saw firsthand how the non-medical use of pharmaceutical-grade fentanyl could reach out and grab its victim. A colleague training in anesthesiology, who apparently had an opioid use disorder, overdosed on fentanyl and nearly died. A suspicious peer had seen the anesthesiologist-in-training enter the bathroom but not leave. Rumors about the anesthesiologist-in-training recently returning from a stint in drug rehab had circulated through the hospital. Security was called, and the bathroom door was smashed open with an ax taken from the fire extinguisher cabinet. Emergency medical personnel rescued the anesthesiologist, who had stopped breathing, from certain death. Campbell believes that a dose of Narcan was given to his colleague as an overdose reversal agent.

That drug overdose drama is all too familiar for friends and family of those battling opioid addiction. It is repeated every day across the country. But now, instead of the diversion of pharmaceutical-grade fentanyl from a hospital pharmacy or anesthesiology workroom, illicitly manufactured fentanyl has flooded the world's drug market.

The opioid crisis that has overrun the United States in the last two-and-a-half decades was kick-started by Purdue Pharma's introduction and egregious marketing campaign promoting OxyContin, a longer-acting version of oxycodone. As the crisis transitioned through other formulations of oxycodone, heroin, and fentanyl, it became increasingly lethal. But it all goes back to the spark lit by Purdue Pharma with a marketing plan to sell a Schedule II narcotic like it was ibuprofen or acetaminophen.

As OxyContin became a blockbuster success, the body count started piling up. The death rate from drug overdoses in the United States more than tripled between 1999 and 2017, and opioid overdose deaths increased almost sixfold during the same period.[96] In 2014, life expectancy in the U.S. began dropping for four consecutive years, despite spending the most on healthcare per capita than any other country in the world.[97] American life expectancy is now at its lowest levels since 1996.[98] Today, millions of Americans are addicted to opioids and an average of 223 people die a day from an overdose—more deaths than a 737 passenger airliner crashing into the sea every day.[99] In 2022, the CDC estimated 107,477 overall drug overdose deaths in the U.S., with around 75 percent of them caused by opioids.[100] This means that more people in the United States now die from overdoses involving opioids than from car accidents, gun deaths, or HIV/AIDS-related illnesses at the peak of the AIDS epidemic.[101]

No Purdue Pharma executives have ever been incarcerated for their role in creating the opioid epidemic. In 2020, the company pleaded guilty to three felony counts of criminal wrongdoing, including violations of the federal anti-kickback law for paying doctors through its speaker program to write more OxyContin prescriptions. Dr. Campbell sat through one such program at a steakhouse with a few colleagues. It was basically a scientific and clinical lecture by a pain management expert, followed by a question-and-answer session. But just like its 2007 plea deal with federal prosecutors, Purdue Pharma's 2020 guilty plea did not bring with it orange jumpsuits or pairs of handcuffs. Instead, the company agreed to pay $3.54 billion in criminal fines and $2 billion in criminal forfeiture of profits. In addition, the Sackler family agreed to pay $225 million out of their estimated net worth of at least $13 billion.[102]

Although Purdue Pharma was able to settle its latest federal criminal case, the Sackler family is not out of the woods. In an attempt to settle thousands of civil lawsuits, the Sacklers reached a deal in March 2022 with attorneys general for eight states and the District of Columbia to pay up to $6 billion in cash. The settlement removed the family from control over the company, although they admitted no wrongdoing. As part of the agreement, Purdue Pharma declared bankruptcy with the intent of reorganizing into a public benefit company, Knoa Pharma LLC. The new entity will be owned by the National Opioid Abatement Trust, an entity controlled by the company's creditors, so that profits from future opioid sales can fund its current and future civil liabilities.[103]

The new public benefit company will help pay off its domestic debts and penalties in the United States by selling their drugs, including OxyContin and addiction-reversal medication, overseas at great profit. In other words, the company will export America's opioid epidemic overseas to help reimburse local governments for the costs of the carnage the company created at home. And in an ironic twist, the new public benefit company could entangle states in the operation of Purdue Pharma's opioid business that they sued and attempted to shut down.[104]

Legal wrangling over Purdue Pharma continues. On June 27, 2024, the U.S. Supreme Court rejected the company's bankruptcy agreement because it offered the Sacklers—who did not declare bankruptcy themselves—unusually broad protection from opioid-related civil claims. In a 5–4 decision, the Supreme Court agreed with the U.S. government's argument that such a deal would give the Sacklers an "exceptional and unprecedented" release "from every conceivable type of opioid-related civil claim—even claims based on fraud and other forms of willful misconduct that could not be discharged if the Sacklers filed for bankruptcy in their individual capacities."[105]

Writing for the majority, Justice Neil Gorsuch echoed the bankruptcy trustee's hope that "there may be a better deal on the horizon" and noted that "[t]he Sacklers have not filed for bankruptcy and have not placed virtually all their assets on the table for distribution to creditors, yet they seek what essentially amounts to a discharge."[106]

During Purdue Pharma's heyday, its heavy-handed marketing tactics generated billions in revenues and pushed patients to the brink, with Florida's libertarian climate providing safe haven for the nation's opioid dealers. After the state finally shut down the unregulated purveyors of pain pills, the new growth industry became drug treatment centers and sober homes, fueled in part by new mandated insurance coverage for substance use disorders. South Florida's warm, sunny beaches and existing pool of addiction treatment centers became a magnet for those looking for recovery and sobriety. Healthcare providers who had lost their moral compass led drug-addicted people in the throes of a disease of the brain to the revolving door of treatment centers, some of them corrupted, others struggling in a challenging healthcare system. Medical insurance fraud was the foundation of the Florida Shuffle, building a prison, and often handing down a life sentence, to the victims of addiction.

Health insurers in Florida developed models for addiction treatment. One of those became widely known as the "Florida Model." That model is a stepwise progression from highly intense treatment through decreasing supervision aimed at preparing the recovering substance use disorder patient to avoid relapse by developing and maintaining the life skills needed to thrive. At least, that is the Florida Model in theory. In reality, the inherent flaws of the Florida Model have created fertile ground for the Florida Shuffle.

CHAPTER 5

THE FLORIDA MODEL

There are many clinical manifestations of substance use disorder. They range from obsessions, compulsions, ruminations, impulsivity, disinterest, and indecision. Then there are the actions that plague those in the throes of substance use disorder. Stealing, hiding, sleeping too much or too little, arguing, tremors, doctor shopping, medicine cabinet thievery, and acquiring new like-minded friends to share these behaviors, while distancing oneself from old friends and family members, are all too common. The cravings of addiction, which is the severe form of substance use disorder, are notoriously profound and uncontrollable, leading to reckless behavior without regard to adverse consequences or the well-being of others.

More than anything else, however, the overwhelming compulsion to use more drug is to keep from being "dopesick," rather than just to get high. In her powerful 2018 bestseller, *Dopesick*, Beth Macy spoke with two aging opioid addicts in the Midwest, Debbie Honaker and Crystal Street:

They'd both lost their teeth. "You get sick and throw up. Or you leave pills in your mouth, and it takes the enamel off," Honaker said. Neither had ever worked steadily. "You couldn't keep a job because you'd steal if you worked at a restaurant," Street added. "Or you just couldn't get up and go—you were too sick." Honaker put in, "At the end of your journey, you're not going after drugs to get high; you're going to keep from being sick."[107]

Overcoming addiction is never easy, as the reward centers of the brain remain rewired for a long time. Many have described to us how they hang on to sobriety by the tips of their fingers, taking each day one at a time. The risk of relapse is already high without exploitation by illegal patient-brokering, unscrupulous marketing tactics, health insurance fraud, and myriad financial crimes. In the 1970s, methadone treatment was the mainstay for medical treatment of opioid use disorder. Abstinence-based programs, often called twelve-step or sobriety programs, including Narcotics Anonymous, have remained part of the portfolio of organized addiction treatment for decades.

In the United States today, the drug treatment space is decentralized and largely privatized. In Palm Beach County, the largest mental health provider is the county jail. When worried parents tell us about their homeless child's addiction and drug-related arrest, we assure them that the county jail is safer than living on the streets and offers an opportunity to detox and get clean.

There is no universally adopted method to heal the brain from a substance use disorder. Although abstinence-only programs can be helpful for those with alcohol use disorder, they are less compatible with the harsh reality of an opioid addiction. Medication-assisted treatment, known as MAT, uses evidence-based drug therapy, often combined with cognitive-behavioral therapy for a better chance of achieving a lasting recovery. In particular, the medications recognized by the scientific and medical community as effective in treating opioid addiction are buprenorphine, naltrexone, and methadone.[108]

Sadly, only around 15 percent of Americans aged twelve or older with a substance use disorder receive treatment of any kind.[109] Among those with an opioid use disorder, only around 18 percent received MAT,[110] even though there is proof that using MAT reduces the death rate among addicted populations by over 50 percent.[111] One explanation for the underutilization of MAT is concern among providers and advocates over issues of cost and compliance, and trepidation about replacing one drug for another.

In SAMHSA's 2022 national survey on drug use, government researchers found that 95 percent of adults who did not receive treatment for their substance use disorder believed they did not need treatment. That figure rises to 97.5 percent for adolescents aged twelve to seventeen with a substance use disorder. Whether it is denial, fear of stigma, or other reasons, there remains a significant unmet need for drug treatment among a large majority of those with substance use disorder. [112]

In the Florida Model of drug rehab, as displayed in the diagram that follows, detox and inpatient care last as long as insurance will pay for it, which is normally one to two weeks. Then the patient usually moves to outpatient care, which involves urinalysis testing and group counseling. Insurance pays for the outpatient treatment component for about six weeks but does not pay for housing. That's where the sober home comes in as, ideally, a reasonably priced group residence that's supervised, drug-free, and conducive to recovery. Residents generally pay by the week, which can be a challenge for those with no job, savings, or family to foot the bill. After the insurance runs out on the outpatient treatment, the patient hopefully has recovered and can return home to restart his or her life.

The Florida Model IN THEORY

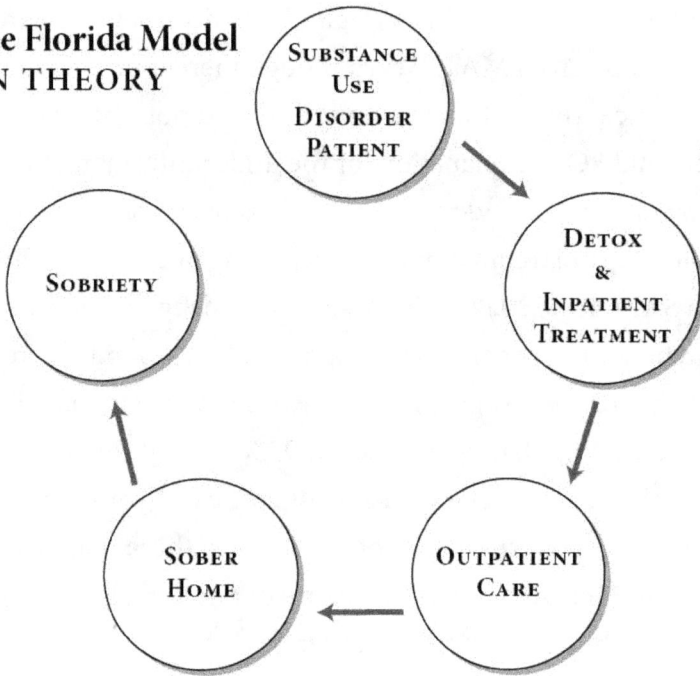

SUBSTANCE USE DISORDER PATIENT

DETOX & INPATIENT TREATMENT

OUTPATIENT CARE

SOBER HOME

SOBRIETY

FIGURE 1: The Florida Model in Theory

The Florida Model has been around for a long time, created and propagated by health insurance actuaries. It is difficult to determine how much input medical doctors who are addiction specialists have had in the development of this model. But regardless of its origins, the model is built for failure. Substance use disorder is often a chronic and persistent illness, yet private insurance traditionally pays for unlimited cycles of short-term, acute rehab with only about a 10 percent success rate. Studies have shown that a more effective approach is to provide longer, decelerated care: a recovery over twelve months has proven cheaper and more successful than an unending series of seven- to twenty-one-day inpatient stays followed by intensive outpatient treatment for six to eight weeks, all marked by overtesting and overbilling.[113]

The lack of housing in the Florida Model has contributed to its failure and increased the rates of fraud and abuse. Other than short stints in detox and inpatient care, patients are on their own to find and pay for places to stay while in rehab. Moreover, unlike drug treatment centers—which are regulated by state and federal laws designed to ensure safety and quality—sober homes are largely unregulated. Fears of lawsuits under the Americans with Disabilities Act (ADA) and Federal Housing Amendments Act (FHAA) have paralyzed states and local governments from attempting effective oversight. Insurance companies do not pay for such housing, so their anti-fraud divisions have no leverage over sober homes and no interest in what occurs behind their closed doors. Over the years, the ADA has protected the rights of the disabled against discrimination but now is being misused as a shield by rogue owners of sober homes who harm their residents for financial gain.

In 2017, Delray Beach Mayor Cary Glickstein told reporters he had no way of knowing the number of sober homes and their residents in his city because of the lax oversight. He estimated that in Delray Beach, a city of 66,000 residents, about 700 sober homes were operating back then, housing around 7,000 people in recovery. Most of those living in sober homes, then and now, are young adults. To the mayor, bad sober homes were crowding out the good ones: "These kids are just cycled through different houses," Glickstein said. "There's no real supervision. Many times, they're supervised by convicted felons, people that are trafficking drugs while they're supposed to be supervising kids in recovery. It's a tragedy on so many levels," said Glickstein. "The desperate parents in Ohio and Kentucky and Michigan that are being lured through deceptive websites with palm trees have no idea what their kids are getting into when they get down here."[114]

Recovering opioid addicts who live in sober homes with others battling the same brain disease are easily manipulated for nefarious purposes. That is why patient brokering, a predatory practice that targets this vulnerable population, is so heinous. Patient brokering occurs when a healthcare facility pays a third party, usually called a marketer, to procure patients. It is illegal to pay a kickback or a bribe or split fees to get a patient.[115] Facilities are allowed to hire marketers, but they can't be paid based on volume. Put more starkly, patient brokering occurs when a rehab pays a body broker to put a head in a bed.

It is a crime because healthcare decisions should be based on what gets a patient well, not what gets people rich. Patient brokering skews the healthcare system to siphon money to corrupt providers who do not have the patient's interests at heart. The results are poor outcomes, excessive readmission rates, and skyrocketing healthcare costs.

Because of a lack of housing and the profitability of patient brokering, what was designed as a theoretical model of recovery has, in practice, become a model for relapse. The diagram below illustrates how the Florida Model became the Florida Shuffle.

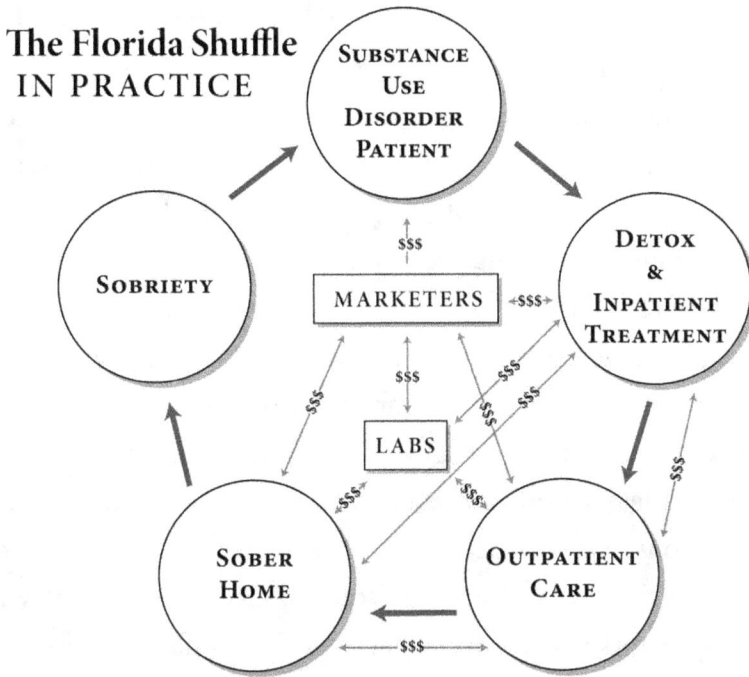

FIGURE 2: "The Florida Shuffle"—in Practice

It usually starts with deceptive marketing practices to con-vince prospective patients or their parents to choose Florida as their destination for drug rehab. The marketers communicate through the internet or on the telephone and offer induce-ments—such as a free plane ticket, complimentary transporta-tion, and co-ed living arrangements—to a rehab center. Quality living arrangements nuzzled up to picturesque beaches, warm weather, and palm trees swaying in the breeze are tough to turn down. Once the hook is set, the marketers reel in the prey.

In the Florida Shuffle, the marketer directs individuals with substance use disorder—often an opioid addiction, which includes fentanyl, heroin, oxycodone and others, as well as il-licit substances like cocaine and methamphetamine, to name a few—to detox and inpatient care facilities to gain sobriety. After those inpatient insurance benefits expire, they transition to an intensive outpatient program chosen by a marketer who collects an illegal commission for the referral. Since health insurance covers outpatient treatment but not housing, patients often live in sober homes, with an average rent of around $200 a week. Sober homes, also known as "recovery residences," are designed as group housing for those in treatment. Residents pay rent out of their own pockets since they are not medical facilities or treatment centers and are not eligible for insurance reimbursements.

In an ideal world, the sober home is a supportive, drug-free environment with active supervision and attentive owners. Unfortunately, the reality of easy money created an industry of shady operators and crooked marketers who offer free rent and other illegal benefits as long as the residents attend a complicit outpatient treatment center, which provides kickbacks to the sober home. The residents, meanwhile, are often willing victims, receiving dirt cheap housing and free transportation until their insurance policies run out. Because of federal law, however, the health insurance coverage must restart when the resident relapses, which is encouraged by the heartless manipulators in this scheme, and the cycle begins again.

It is not just the illegal kickbacks and free gifts that make a sober home corrupt, but also the substandard living conditions. A marketer never lures a prospect with promises of a sleazy flophouse. Survivors of the Florida Shuffle often describe the horror of moving into a home far different than its flowery description, where drug use is commonplace, prostitution is baked into the system, filth covers every exposed surface, bed bugs and cockroaches share the bedrooms and kitchen with people, and infectious diseases run rampant. Sometimes, a resident will overdose and die from the illegal substances that the sober home ostensibly was designed to ward off.

John Lehman, former executive director of the Florida Association of Recovery Residences (FARR), condemns the corrupt players in his industry for this "predatory model, where it's not about patient care and outcomes." Instead, Lehman labels it "a revenue source" where "the insurance card in the kid's wallet is going to be milked for every penny it's worth." He notes that treatment providers work with unethical sober home operators to "offer the kid free room and board, free transportation, and free other stuff because they're in competition with other predatory providers. Sometimes, they must up the ante to keep him: cell phones and scooters and nicer properties on the intracoastal with jet skis." As to where the money comes from to pay for all these illegal perks, Lehman says "the answer is they'll over-utilize urinalysis testing."[116]

Indeed, unscrupulous owners of rogue sober homes receive hundreds of dollars per resident per day in illegal kickbacks from outpatient rehab centers that conduct excessive tests and unproven treatments that are all reimbursed by insurance companies on a fee-for-service basis under the ACA.

It is sad but not unusual for a vulnerable victim of substance use disorder to achieve recovery in a drug rehab program, only to relapse later. It is a travesty, however, when this occurs at the hands of a provider driven by greed. The previous diagram shows how illegal kickbacks and patient brokering infect the Florida Model of rehab and have led to the relapse and ultimate death of so many who sought help, only to be exploited for possessing the very insurance benefits that were supposed to provide a way out. In fact, the only bubble in the diagram that is not profitable is "sobriety."

All the participants of the Florida Shuffle receive a financial windfall at the expense of U.S. taxpayers and other insurance policyholders. When not satisfied with receiving illegal kickbacks from marketers, outpatient treatment centers, and labs, some sober homes have aggressively attempted to work with corrupt providers to conduct medical treatments in the hope of sharing in the insurance largesse. In the July 2020 arrest report for Michael Ligotti, DO, the notorious rehab doctor who was "treating" Jamie Daniels in Delray Beach, the FBI stated: "In recent years, some sober homes have seized upon the opportunity to bill insurance companies and have entered into agreements with medical providers (such as LIGOTTI) who purport to offer primary care to residents. Those providers may also authorize testing to be conducted at the sober home or billed by laboratories for such sober home patients."[117]

Chief Assistant State Attorney Alan Johnson, who oversees Palm Beach County's Sober Homes Task Force, explains that "needing a place to live is the key ingredient that distinguishes the Florida Model from other recovery models in other areas of the country," he said. "You have people who are away from home in intensive forms of outpatient treatment. They need housing. If the housing is corrupt, they feed into this cycle of relapse over recovery."[118]

CHAPTER 6

A COMMUNITY FIGHTS BACK

The morning sun had barely peeked over the horizon east of Palm Beach as mosquitoes relentlessly attacked the first group of attorneys in business attire, walking with a purpose toward the massive grey stone courthouse. Men and women qualified by the Florida Bar trudged toward the bastion of justice with leather briefcases hanging at their sides, or rolling with the clank, clank, clank of cheap plastic wheels hitting cracks and crevices in the decades-old concrete sidewalk. Their clients, with far more skin exposed, were slowly sauntering, seemingly without purpose, as if they could take back the events that led them to this day of justice. Many looked furtively here and there out of habits long engrained by days and nights on the streets of Palm Beach County.

Just to the north sat a smaller building made of the same cold, grey stone, looking empty and forlorn as all the pedestrians headed the other way toward the courthouse. It was the Office of the State Attorney for the Fifteenth Judicial Circuit in downtown West Palm Beach. It was the seat of law enforcement power in a county that had the ignominious distinction as the epicenter of the Florida Shuffle, the collection of criminal behaviors in a corrupted drug rehab and sober home industry that promoted relapse over recovery. The building was rather like the Alamo, with far more perpetrators and victims outside the stone walls than the number of crusaders, prosecutors, and humanitarians inside. The difference was, instead of Mexican troops under President General Santa Anna wanting to reclaim the mission, the Florida Shuffle's "perps" and willing victims wanted nothing to do with those walls, or the law enforcement officials within them.

On the third floor of the six-story building, inside a spartan government office with the monotony of never-ending beige walls interrupted only by a random plaque or framed picture, sat Ted Padich, the chief investigator for the country's first and only Sober Homes Task Force. With a trademark cop mustache, now fully grey after forty-two years in law enforcement, Padich's reputation as a respected, relentless sleuth earned him the right to wear his favored Hawaiian shirts to work—an ironic wardrobe choice for a grizzled veteran of Florida's shady underbelly.

The road that led Padich to the Office of the State Attorney, Dave Aronberg, began in 2015 when Aronberg met with civic leaders from the city of Delray Beach to discuss their pleas for help to combat the rise of rogue sober homes throughout the fifteen square-miles of their eclectic city. Delray Beach has had a long-established drug treatment industry—in 2007, the *New York Times* described it as "the epicenter of the country's largest and most vibrant recovery community"[119]—but generous new federal laws that expanded insurance benefits had attracted predators with dollar signs in their eyes to descend upon the city.

Aronberg and his team of prosecutors understood the gravity of the situation but told the group that local prosecutors were hamstrung as well. His office could go it alone while Washington slept, but, at minimum, his prosecutors needed the Florida legislature to provide new laws and additional resources to take meaningful action.

The goal at the end of the meeting was to convince the conservative, anti-regulation Florida legislature to pass new laws with tougher penalties against fraud and abuse in the drug treatment and sober home industries. This was not an easy task.

In 2016, Palm Beach County legislators developed a proposed bill to address the corruption in the rehab business. But as expected, the measure stalled upon its introduction. The chairman of the first committee hearing the bill in the Florida House of Representatives, Rep. Jason Brodeur, a Republican from the Orlando area, asked why new statewide laws were needed to address a distinctly Palm Beach County problem. He told the bill sponsors that State Attorney Aronberg and his prosecutors should target the fraud and abuse at the local level by starting a task force.

When Aronberg heard of Chairman Brodeur's alternative proposal of a task force in lieu of any new legislation, Aronberg agreed—but only if it was done correctly, which required a one-time appropriation of funds from the legislature. Knowing firsthand that the Republican-dominated Florida legislature was normally reluctant to send money to pet projects in Democratic counties such as Palm Beach, Aronberg challenged Brodeur and his colleagues to provide a non-recurring grant of $250,000 to start a task force with a full-time prosecutor, forensic accountant, and lead investigator. To keep costs down, Aronberg said that he would ask law enforcement agencies from throughout the county to loan investigators to the task force, rather than hire additional personnel.

For prosecutors, a task force can be a powerful vehicle to fight crime. Normally, prosecutors get cases only after they are first investigated and vetted by a police agency. For example, in the television show *Law & Order*, the police who investigate crimes are depicted in the first half-hour, followed by the prosecutors in the second half of the show. In a task force, prosecutors move to join police in the first half. Rather than await the results of a law enforcement investigation, prosecutors are proactive and work with police to find the criminal conduct and hold the wrongdoers accountable.

With Rep. Brodeur's support, and with the strong advocacy of the Palm Beach County legislative delegation, the Florida legislature in 2016 gave State Attorney Aronberg's office $275,000 to start a Sober Homes Task Force—which was even $25,000 more than Aronberg had requested. The goals were lofty: clean up the drug treatment industry in Palm Beach County and issue a report on what the Florida legislature needed to do on a statewide basis. Although Palm Beach County's sought-after legislation was rejected, the Florida legislature gave Aronberg's office a year to show real progress and to recommend any necessary changes to state law in time for the 2017 legislative session. Meanwhile, in 2016, Delray Beach paramedics responded to 748 drug overdoses; most involved opioids, with sixty-five of them ending in death.[120]

Aronberg immediately reached out to the Palm Beach County

sheriff and the police chiefs from several local law enforcement agencies to request investigators for the law enforcement side of the task force. That first step begged the question: Who would be the top investigator to lead such an unprecedented effort to fight an emerging crisis? Without any playbook to follow, Aronberg appointed Chief Assistant State Attorney Alan Johnson—who had expressed an interest in this area—as the lead prosecutor. But choosing the lead investigator would be a tougher decision, as the individual would have to be found outside Aronberg's office in the world of law enforcement.

Aronberg's prosecutors repeatedly mentioned the name of Ted Padich, who was a captain within Florida's Division of Insurance Fraud (DIF). Since the Florida Shuffle is, at its core, a virulent strain of insurance fraud, Padich had been looking into allegations of corruption within the drug treatment industry. It was an open secret, however, that Padich was frustrated at the lack of cases filed by state and federal prosecutors.

Padich, who had worked for the Boynton Beach Police Department for twenty-one years before joining DIF in 1999, was one of the first to sound the alarm about the emerging fraud within the drug treatment sector. Padich spoke with Dr. Campbell in a series of interviews from September 2020 through July 2022. "In late 2013, I was a lieutenant for DIF in West Palm Beach focused primarily on mortgage fraud," said Padich, "when a woman walked into our office with a suspicion that something was afoul at her workplace." Padich recalled that the woman was a licensed massage therapist when an old acquaintance, who was a trained hypnotist, came back into her life with a business proposal. In the past, the woman said she doubted the man's trustworthiness, but now he seemed sincere about wanting to start a wellness company with her in Delray Beach. The business plan appeared sound, so she decided to give it a try.

"On the grand opening in their new subleased office space, a young man with a backpack appeared, holding a skateboard in one hand and a cup of urine in the other," said Padich. "He wanted $25." The woman thought he was probably looking for the doctor next door who was their landlord—until he mentioned her business partner's name. Padich said, "The kid then left his urine and said he'd come back later."

By the end of the day, the woman reported that forty different people came by to demand $25 for their urine samples. Believing that her business partner was likely involved in some sort of fraud, the woman called him to demand an explanation. His response was that he sometimes helped out insurance companies by "collecting" urine for them. This confirmed all her doubts about her business partner's character, so the woman returned the office key to the landlord next door, left the urine samples on the desk, and never looked back. The new business enterprise ended on the day it started.

"Around that time, we were starting to get word of an increase in drug overdoses around the county," Padich said, "but I didn't put two and two together yet. About two weeks later, a licensed drug counselor in Delray Beach called me to report a drug treatment facility that offered no therapy." Padich recounted that the counselor was incensed that all she was doing was "collecting urine from these kids who were doing nothing but smoking cigarettes, drinking Red Bull, playing ping pong and watching TV. The woman earned a degree to try to help people, but instead was just a urine collector."

In response, Padich reached out to every insurance company in his database to find out if they experienced any such fraud. Yet not a single insurer reported a problem. Refusing to accept the industry's Pollyanna denials, Padich and his detectives visited a urine testing lab in Delray Beach to discover a shocking sight: "There were so many kids waiting to give urine that there were employees with clipboards and whistles keeping them in line," Padich recalled.

Soon thereafter, with overdose deaths rising and, according to Padich, sober homes opening "in every neighborhood," the health insurance carriers started to report massive fraud. "So much fraud was now being reported, we stopped counting at half-a-billion dollars. From early 2014 to 2017, we logged at least three hundred complaints, yet DIF only gave me one detective to investigate it. My immediate supervisor in Broward County didn't want to hear of it, and I was constantly berated for wasting time on these investigations, even after all these kids were coming down to Florida to die."

A major part of the problem was the DIF bureaucracy, which was not on the ground in Delray Beach, or even Palm Beach County. As Padich agonized over the dramatic rise in insurance fraud and, more importantly, the loss of life, his immediate supervisor was stationed in a neighboring county that had not yet been affected by the Florida Shuffle. The top bosses, meanwhile, were ensconced in DIF's headquarters more than four hundred miles away in Tallahassee.

Another issue was the DIF quota. Whether for politics or public relations or both, DIF still requires that every detective file a minimum of eleven fraud cases a year to the local state attorney. This ensures an impressive total case count in a state that has an abundance of insurance fraud. But at the same time, a quota discourages detectives from investigating large cases, such as the Florida Shuffle's massive fraud. "Any investigator could file eleven small cases of auto insurance fraud *every month* if they wanted to, but if you're a gifted investigator seeking to root out major corruption in the drug treatment industry, it could cost you your job," said Padich. "That's because a single case of drug treatment fraud worth many millions can take six months or longer to investigate, with dozens of leads, interviews, and hundreds of bank records to review."

Padich refused to let his supervisor or DIF's quota system dissuade him from advocating for more investigators and more resources to battle this growing scourge within his community. There is, however, a price to be paid for being an agitator inside a top-down bureaucracy. "I was being berated by my supervisor for speaking out and knew my days were numbered inside the Division of Insurance Fraud," said Padich. "I was beside myself because I knew that we could do something about these fraud cases, and with a half-dozen good detectives, we could make a dent in the death toll. It was about then when I received the call from Chief Assistant Alan Johnson, who told me about the new task force."

A face-to-face meeting ensued, where Johnson offered Padich the position with the State Attorney's Office. Although this meant a salary cut from his old job, Padich accepted immediately and enthusiastically. "Frankly, it was a dream come true," he said. "It gave me an opportunity to end my career the same way I started it: by helping people and having a real impact."

From the moment he started as the chief investigator, Padich went full steam ahead. It stuck in his craw that young people would be enticed to Padich's home county under false pretenses for drug treatment, only to be dehumanized and commoditized for their insurance benefits. He has been answering the Task Force hotline since it started in 2016, helping parents from all over the country locate and rescue their loved ones, and has also consoled scores of desperate parents after it was too late.

"After parents realize that something has gone wrong," Padich said. "They make an exhaustive series of phone calls lasting several weeks, and finally call me by finding the phone number for the Sober Homes Task Force. You cannot believe the number of desperate family members I have spent hundreds of hours talking to about their son or daughter who disappeared into a black hole without any communication from the less-than-reputable facilities."

"Part of the problem faced by parents with addicted children is the lack of research they do into the facility they are entrusting with their loved one's life," Padich said. "After finding an addiction treatment facility and sending their child south to Florida, it only takes a few weeks until they often realize there is a problem." Padich explained that the family members usually cannot get through to anybody at the facility. The parents call police in South Florida who provide "zero help," he said. "Then, they call every state bureaucrat and politician they can find—and they too are no help. Now even more desperate, the middle-aged parent with a young adult child incommunicado in a drug treatment facility or sober living home goes to their local cops, such as in

New York, New Jersey or Connecticut. And of course, those local law enforcement officials cannot help. It is not their jurisdiction. It is not even their state."

According to Padich, a common scenario involves parents who send their problem child to drug rehab to get him or her away from the family. They may have two or three other children under the same roof, and when one of them is addicted to opioids, and often involving many different drugs (polypharmacy), domestic tranquility is out the window. He has become disruptive to the family. She is a discipline problem. He steals, lies, drops out of college and cannot find employment. At their wits end, parents typically go online and rely on advertisements to choose a rehab facility. Unfortunately, there is no truth in advertising among thieves. Padich has seen kids get off planes at Palm Beach International Airport with saddles, believing they will use them for horseback riding during treatment. Others have checked their golf clubs because shady marketers promised them eighteen holes a day. Some have the mistaken belief that they'll be riding around on jet skis and taking yacht trips, rather than feeling dopesick during withdrawal from their drug of choice.

The Florida Shuffle's new recruits are almost always sent to a rundown location for substandard rehab by way of a shuttle, pejoratively nicknamed the "druggie buggy." The buggy is usually a big white passenger van that serves as a favorite for churches, soccer teams, and drug rehab centers. Some of the newbies described being plopped into insect-infested shabby or dreary houses and treated badly by the owners or operators from the very beginning. But now they are trapped by their circumstances. They burned bridges back home, have no money, no job, and do not have friends or family in town to fall back on. They are still using drugs or suffering through dopesickness from withdrawal. As their bodies are enveloped by such searing pains, they are emotionally fragile and exceptionally vulnerable.

Padich spoke with one mother about her drug-addicted daughter. The mother told him her daughter had been lying to her for two years, had been stealing from the family, and thwarted every effort to help her shake her addictions. The mother sent her daughter to Florida as a last resort. After a brief stint in an inpatient drug rehabilitation facility, she was transferred to outpatient therapy, and sent to live in a local sober home that was in cahoots with the drug rehab facility. Within twenty-four hours, the daughter called her mother to complain that her room had roaches, bedbugs, and rats. She described where she was as a filthy slum in a dangerous neighborhood.

With each passing day, the mother heard more horror stories but told her desperate and disgruntled daughter to get better because this was tough love. She told her to buckle up and do what she was told. Day after day, the daughter called until finally the mother flew to Florida to see for herself if the complaints were true. Given the history of lies and thievery, she assumed her untrustworthy daughter was embellishing and she would find a tidy, quaint home in a lovely neighborhood with flowers, palm trees, and a Starbucks down the street. She just wanted to prove her problem-child daughter wrong.

Indeed, one of them was wrong. But it was not the daughter. Once the mother drove to the facility from the airport, she found a rundown motel in a depressed part of town. Her daughter's room was filthy. Indeed, it was infested with vermin. As the story unfolded on the telephone, the detective's heart sank. Padich knew where this conversation was going. He had heard the narrative at least three hundred times in the past four years.

Her voice dropped as she told Padich that she was too late. Her daughter had already relapsed, overdosed on drugs, and died. All she could do was collect her belongings, identify her beloved daughter's body at the county medical examiner's building, and make the arrangements to transport her home for a funeral.

Padich has seen a seemingly endless flow of parents from out of state put their children on a plane for drug rehab far from home where they cannot check on them. They cannot verify anything their son or daughter says. Some parents are so frustrated that they send their addicted child to Palm Beach County on a whim, based on an online post.

"Some people spend more time buying a car than selecting a rehab facility for their child," Padich lamented. "You would never pick a medical facility for your cancer based on a Facebook ad alone. But mental health is still seen as different and is widely misunderstood."

As word spread about the Sober Homes Task Force, Aronberg was flooded by requests from people in the rehab industry who wanted to participate. Appreciating the potential of a group of industry insiders—including the possibility of some of the ne'er-do-wells—offering up their secrets and providing intelligence on wrongdoing and wrongdoers, Aronberg created a separate part of the Task Force that was open to anyone with a sincere interest in assisting his efforts. Since Aronberg had spent eight years in the world of politics as a state senator, he didn't like to tell eager volunteers no. The community side of the Task Force kept expanding until he finally had to cap it at forty members.

At the first community Task Force meeting, Alan Johnson shocked the room when he stood up and announced that all financial incentives provided to current and prospective patients were *illegal*. Drug treatment centers and sober homes could not provide clients with free plane tickets to their facilities, free or reduced rent at their sober homes, or even free food and drink. "Even a free pack of cigarettes would constitute illegal patient brokering in violation of Florida law," said Johnson, not mentioning that Florida law was so weak that it took thirteen separate counts of patient brokering to qualify a defendant for prison time.

The gasps inside the conference room were audible. Exclaimed one stunned rehab owner: "But that's standard in the industry!" Johnson then told the dispirited attendees that just because this was long the accepted way of doing business, it was not, in fact, acceptable.

"The next time you're caught driving ninety miles per hour on the highway," said Johnson, "try telling the cop that you were just going the same speed as everyone else. See how well that works!" In an instant, the community Task Force members and guests in attendance understood, although many still didn't like it. Change would be sudden, could be difficult, but was definitely necessary.

Some members of the community side of the Task Force thought that their participation would insulate their own conduct from criminal liability. They attended meetings and then used their participation on the Task Force to market themselves as some of the good guys in the industry. Unfortunately for them,

Padich's side of the Task Force gave no "get out of jail free" cards to participants who continued to sully the drug treatment industry by trafficking in patients, committing insurance fraud, or providing illegal benefits or kickbacks. As time went on, pictures would speak louder than words. It sent a chill down the spine of rehab operators who continued to live on the edge when they started to see colleagues who had recently attended a Task Force meeting now wearing a pair of handcuffs.

After months of lengthy meetings, the civilian side of the Task Force drafted legislation that the Florida legislature then passed into law in 2017. This would dramatically transform Florida's weak laws on patient brokering and treatment center oversight into the strongest rules of their kind in the country. In addition to tightened enforcement of rogue rehabs and increased industry regulation, the State Attorney's Office empaneled a grand jury to consider additional reforms. Months later, the grand jury issued a report that included a critical section on Google's practice of selling its search words for rehab marketing to the highest bidder, regardless of whom that was. In response, Google changed the way it ranks search results for drug treatment centers and now requires all providers to first be vetted by an independent third-party certification service, LegitScript, before they can advertise on the search engine. Soon thereafter, Facebook followed Google's lead.

Three years after its inception, with Ted Padich leading the charge, the Sober Homes Task Force made its 99th and 100th arrests for patient brokering, nabbing two executives of a Pennsylvania medical lab. The defendants paid more than $3 million in illegal kickbacks to brokers in exchange for urine samples that were collected from recovering addicts living in sober homes throughout Palm Beach County. Meanwhile, Padich's previous employer—the state agency tasked by law to investigate and combat insurance fraud—has made only one arrest relating to the Florida Shuffle and is no longer an active participant in the Sober Homes Task Force.

CHAPTER 7

THE ONE THAT GOT AWAY

The Sober Homes Task Force's aim has never been to banish those battling substance use disorder, or to shut down legitimate sober homes and drug treatment centers. Treatment of addiction is a valued component of the healthcare system and is a crucial part of overcoming the opioid epidemic. The ongoing focus of the Task Force is to eliminate the bad players and bad practices, not to be a zoning or code enforcement authority.[121]

By the end of 2023, the Task Force had made 121 arrests and, despite a pause in trials due to the pandemic, achieved 110 convictions with more to come. The Palm Beach County Medical Examiner validated the crackdown on patient brokering and insurance fraud, revealing that opioid overdose deaths decreased by 33 percent between 2017 and 2021. In addition, according to the Florida Medical Examiners Commission, the county experienced a 17 percent decrease in opioid overdose deaths in 2023, compared to a statewide decrease of 3 percent.[122] Another encouraging statistic from Palm Beach County is a stunning 56 percent reduction in fire-rescue transports for suspected drug overdoses between 2017 and 2023.[123]

One high-profile arrest during the Task Force crackdown involved an undercover investigation of Dr. Max Citrin of Boca Raton. "We heard that this doctor from Boca was infamous for writing lots of prescriptions to people in rehab in exchange for recruiting others in recovery to his practice," Padich said. "So, we sent in an undercover officer to get Xanax. The first thing that Citrin's staff did was to administer a skin prick test for allergies because the undercover officer was a new patient, even though she never mentioned having allergy problems. The entire visit took around twenty minutes."[124]

Padich's team waited a few weeks and then spoke to a fraud investigator from Blue Cross Blue Shield (BCBS), which was the health insurance plan billed for the undercover officer's clinical office visit. To everyone's surprise, the BCBS employee said that Citrin billed the insurance company $15,000 for the twenty-minute allergy test and nonexistent treatment. But that was not the biggest shock. The insurance company investigator started looking at the records for Dr. Citrin, who was just thirty-four years old at the time. Padich could hear her frantic clicking of the keyboard right before she let out an audible gasp. Struggling for words, the BCBS employee stammered, "Uh oh . . . Oh my gosh . . . Oh no! He's billed us SEVEN MILLION DOLLARS over the past year!"

Turns out, the brash and brazen Citrin gave prescription drugs to everyone who sought them, and in turn would bill the insurance carriers for fake allergy diagnoses and treatments. Perhaps the worst part, however, was that he copied and pasted the same bogus allergy diagnoses and treatments for hundreds of patients, claiming that black mold exposure from sober homes caused all his patients to have identical ailments.

After scrutinizing the insurance documents, Padich also found that Citrin reported that nearly all his patients had the same exact height, weight, body temperature, and heart rate. And yet, the insurance company dutifully paid every time, even though the fraud was obvious, lazy, and quite expensive. Padich insists that if his investigators had not notified the insurance company of this massive fraud right under their noses, Citrin's criminal enterprise would still be in full swing. Instead, he pleaded guilty in July 2021 to four counts of insurance fraud and was sentenced to thirty months in prison, five years of probation, $2.4 million in restitution, and a forced relinquishment of his medical licenses.[125]

But not even the Citrin case, or any of the other arrests for insurance fraud or patient brokering, could motivate the insurance industry to participate in Palm Beach County's Sober Homes Task Force. "In the early days, we were able to get representatives of various insurance companies to show up once," recalled Alan Johnson, "but they never returned."[126] He was frustrated that even after repeatedly contacting health insurance executives, they always seemed to have something better to do. The monthly Task Force meetings continue to this day without any insurer participation.

The allure of generous insurance payouts with few questions asked attracted many newcomers to the drug treatment industry who were motivated solely by dollar signs. One of them was former Palm Beach Sheriff's Deputy Robert Simeone, a Desert Storm veteran and acquaintance of Dave Aronberg. Simeone left a ten-year career in law enforcement in 2015 to start Epiphany's Treatment Center in West Palm Beach. As a sheriff's deputy,

Simeone had earned a decent side income from a baking business called CopCakes that he operated from his home, but the profits from sugary confections were nothing compared to the margins in the rehab business.

Without any education or training in the treatment field, Simeone was off and running, making around $2 million in his first year. As an industry rookie, Simeone relied on the illegal shortcut of patient brokering to fill his beds, paying more than $200,000 to two local sober-home owners in exchange for referrals. Simeone sent the sober-home owners a weekly fee per client, which decreased if the individual failed to attend the full week of rehab at Epiphany. When one of the sober-home owners learned about Palm Beach County's crackdown on patient brokering and confronted Simeone about the payments, Simeone assured him that "everything was okay," and their agreement was operating in a "gray area."[127], [128]

Simeone did little to hide his brazen kickback scheme, which quickly came to the attention of Aronberg's Sober Homes Task Force. He drove around town in an ostentatious yellow Lamborghini and paid the illegal kickbacks directly from his Epiphany checking account. Some of the checks even listed the specific number of days that the patient attended his treatment programs. Normally, someone who openly flouts the law tries to keep a low profile. Not Robert Simeone. While he was under investigation, he invited additional scrutiny by running for a seat in the Florida House of Representatives, which he lost in 2016.

Sober Homes Task Force investigators first became aware of Simeone after West Palm Beach Police responded to an alleged sexual battery at a sober home named Recovery Rocks, owned by

Terence Dennis. Upon their visit, the officers learned that all the sober home residents went to therapy at Epiphany's Treatment Center. After discussing their suspicions with Padich's team, the Sober Homes Task Force issued a subpoena to Terence Dennis's bank for all checks deposited into his account, which revealed eleven checks from Epiphany.[129]

Meanwhile, in an unrelated case, Padich's investigators took a sworn statement from a local sober-home owner named Alex Vandervert, who admitted to receiving and depositing four checks from Epiphany in exchange for referring clients from his sober home called Saje House. Vandervert said that he had a "handshake agreement" with "Bobby Simeone," whom he identified as the "owner of Epiphany," and admitted that he had never referred patients to Epiphany before getting paid to do so.[130]

After the damning admissions from Vandervert, investigators met with Terence Dennis, who acknowledged that he also received payments from Epiphany in exchange for referring clients of his sober home to the treatment center. Dennis told investigators that his referral fees depended on the clients' insurance: the more generous the insurance policy, the more money Epiphany would give him.[131]

Just two years after Simeone opened Epiphany's doors, Aronberg's prosecutors charged him with twenty-six counts of patient brokering, a third-degree felony under Florida law. After further investigation, prosecutors later increased the charges to fifty counts. Simeone's defense was that his center helped vulnerable adults with substance use disorders, and in any event, he relied on the advice of counsel in this emerging area of the law. On the latter argument, Simeone's legal team hoped to capitalize on a legal motion filed in a different case on whether a lawyer's good faith interpretation of the patient brokering laws could confer immunity on a clients' actions.

Simeone's defense was emboldened in 2019 when a Palm Beach County judge dealt a potentially fatal blow to the Sober Homes Task Force by gutting Florida's anti-patient brokering laws. In a controversial ruling, Judge Laura Johnson turned the old legal maxim that "ignorance of the law is no excuse" on its head by allowing defendants to hide behind their attorney's legal advice, no matter how incorrect. Ruling that "a defendant may assert the advice of counsel defense when charged with violations of the Florida Patient Brokering statute," Judge Johnson offered the infamous get-out-of-jail-free card to all the defendants charged by the Sober Homes Task Force, including Robert Simeone. Prior to Judge Johnson's ruling, Aronberg's prosecutors only had to prove that kickbacks were paid to win a patient brokering case. Now, prosecutors would have to prove that defendants like Simeone knew what they did was illegal, a near-impossible task if the defendant's corporate counsel took the stand to testify in his client's defense.[132]

After Judge Johnson refused to reconsider her devastating decision, Aronberg appealed it to Florida's Fourth District Court of Appeal. Meanwhile, all the Task Force's investigations and prosecutions were put on hold, with the future of the Florida Shuffle crackdown very much in doubt. Lawyers for the State on appeal pointed out that there is no intent element in Florida's Patient Brokering Act, which means prosecutors should not be required to prove that someone knew what they are doing is wrong to be convicted of a crime.

In a unanimous ruling, the appellate court's three-judge panel agreed and reversed Judge Johnson's ruling. Finding that this was a case of first impression, the court held that patient brokering is a "general intent crime, not a specific intent crime," which means "the defendant cannot assert 'advice of counsel' as a defense here." The defendant in the case then appealed to the Florida Supreme Court, which refused to hear the case. It was a huge relief for Aronberg, Padich, Alan Johnson, and the entire Sober Homes Task Force, which overcame a potentially lethal setback to emerge stronger than before. For targets like Robert Simeone, it was "game on."[133]

Unabashed and unashamed while awaiting trial, Simeone collected donations for a charity he previously founded, Children of Wounded Warriors, which ostensibly supported the children of fallen military and police and fire officials. Financial investigators soon discovered, however, that Simeone redirected most of the charity's $73,556 in donations since 2015 into his own personal and business bank accounts. Simeone had promised donors that 80 to 85 percent of donations would go directly into grants for the children "to continue their extracurricular activities that renew their minds and spirits and relieve them of the stress, anxiety, and worry they can experience."[134]

The discovery of Simeone's charity scam led to six more felony charges of organized scheme to defraud, money laundering, and grand theft. The new charges led the judge to revoke his bond on the earlier counts, sending him straight into the Palm Beach County Jail pending trial. The change in accommodations helped convince Simeone to plead guilty to most of the charges, and he is currently serving a five-year prison sentence, to be followed by five years of probation and more than $100,000 in fines and res-titution. He is also barred for life from working in the healthcare, substance abuse treatment, and sober home industries.[135]

Sometimes, the fraud is large enough to attract the attention of the U.S. Department of Justice, as in the case of Dr. Michael Ligotti. For many patients and their advocates, Dr. Ligotti was the human face of the Florida Shuffle, touching nearly every rogue operation in Florida. A notorious Delray Beach physician who served as the medical director for more than fifty differ-ent addiction treatment facilities, Ligotti billed some patients between $10,000 and $20,000 for a single day's visit for fake treatments, redundant urinalyses and blood tests, non-existent therapy sessions, and other unnecessary services. Ligotti did not even review the results of the tests he ordered, as he was the "medical director" in name only. He and his facilities pocketed $121 million for lab testing and other services before the feds, with help from Padich and the Sober Homes Task Force, finally caught up with him.

Federal prosecutors charged Ligotti for his role in the massive scheme that fraudulently billed private insurance and Medicare over $746 million. It remains the largest addiction fraud treat-ment case ever charged by the U.S. Department of Justice. Much of his windfall came from taxpayer funds or private insurance premiums. In October 2022, Ligotti pleaded guilty to conspiracy to commit healthcare fraud and wire fraud, resulting in a twen-ty-year prison sentence and a surrender of his medical license.[136]

Federal prosecutors, however, allowed Ligotti to remain free for the next year to help them build criminal cases against oth-er fraudulent doctors. Ligotti's assistance led to charges against four individuals in Central Florida for healthcare fraud. All four defendants were ultimately acquitted, yet prosecutors and U.S. District Judge Rodolfo Ruiz agreed to cut Ligotti's sentence down to ten years over the objections of two mothers whose children died from Ligotti's greed. One of them was Jamie Daniels' mother, Lisa Daniels-Goldman, who told the court that "Michael Ligotti didn't just steal money from insurance companies. He stole the life of my twenty-three-year-old son, Jamie. Please let Jamie's life mean more than Michael Ligotti's greed."[137]

In contrast with Ligotti's reputation as the godfather of the Florida Shuffle, Boca Raton yoga instructor James Kigar was a relative newbie to the drug treatment world, winning friends and admirers with his sunny disposition and optimistic worldview. As a fit and youthful fifty-four-year-old who prided himself on healthy living, Kigar ventured into the drug treatment business with a facility called Whole Life Recovery in 2015. A year later, as Padich took the helm of Palm Beach County's new Sober Homes Task Force, he kept hearing Kigar's name—and not in a positive way.

The first time Padich heard about Kigar came from a confidential informant who told a Delray Beach detective that Kigar was paying a finder's fee for every insured patient brought to his facility for treatment. The informant, who ran a sober home, received between $400 and $500 per week for each patient. In an apparent attempt to avoid Florida's patient brokering law, Kigar required the informant to complete a "Whole Life Recovery Weekly Individual Case Management Report," even though no one from Whole Life Recovery ever visited his sober home to inspect the living conditions or to verify any of the "case management" services ostensibly provided.[138]

Padich had heard that several treatment facilities were using these case management agreements to get around the prohibition against paying for patients. Florida's patient brokering statute makes it a felony for anyone to "offer or pay a commission, benefit, bonus, rebate, kickback, or bribe, directly or indirectly, in cash or in kind, or engage in any split-fee arrangement, in any form whatsoever, to induce the referral of a patient." If the treatment facility could make it seem that the payments were for legitimate services, and not merely to reward a sober home for sending patients their way, they could evade the letter of the law.[139]

Still, it was enough for Padich to open a Task Force investigation and obtain court approval to conduct an undercover operation at Whole Life. Padich's skepticism over Kigar's business model deepened when he learned that Kigar had hired Christopher Hutson as an operations consultant—a name Padich knew quite well. In 2012, Hutson pleaded guilty to racketeering conspiracy for his role in a notorious pill mill operation that made $40 million in illegal drug sales. Hutson had been released early from his nine-year prison sentence for his cooperation in other cases.[140]

On August 23, 2016, a Whole Life employee called the confidential informant to say that his patient referral fee was ready for pickup. Padich wired up the informant with a hidden recording device and watched him enter the facility. The informant turned in his case management report for each of the patients in his sober home and collected a check. He then sat down for a meeting with Christopher Hutson to ask if he could get more money in exchange for more patients.[141]

Ironically, in the recording, Hutson told the informant that he attends the Sober Homes Task Force meetings to learn "what to expect and what not to do." This led Padich to check the sign-in sheets from the Task Force meetings, and indeed, there was Hutson's name written directly below James Kigar's name on the August 8, 2016, attendee list.[142]

Hutson said that Whole Life would now be using W-2 forms and would make the informant a "bona fide employee with a bonus structure." Under this agreement, the informant would be paid a weekly base salary and a bonus depending on the number of patients sent to the facility. In the hidden recording, Hutson says that Whole Life was "switching to the new format because the State Attorney thought that a sober home referring clients to a treatment facility is considered patient brokering." He said that he and his attorney attended the Task Force meetings twice a month, which convinced him that his company needed to move away from "case management."[143]

As evidence mounted of illegal patient brokering, Padich reached out to former employees of Whole Life. One of them, a former admissions coordinator, told Padich that after a patient attended all of their weekly treatment sessions, Whole Life would pay the sober-home owner the following Tuesday. James Kigar would sign all the company checks, including case management payments, payroll, rent, and any other business checks.[144]

One patient told investigators that she ended up at Whole Life after three men stood in the living room of her sober home and bid on her like ranchers at a cattle auction. Kigar's facility won the bidding war, and the patient was his.[145]

Around the same time, an online review from a "Janet K" accused Whole Life of patient-brokering her daughter:

If you are looking for a safe environment for your young adult to get drug treatment, stay far away from here. My daughter ended up in this place and they set her up in a sober living house with active drug use. The sober living house did not charge my daughter rent as long as she went to the whole life IOP [Intensive Outpatient Program]. This is illegal, but unfortunately happens a lot with less than reputable rehab/sober living homes. My daughter overdosed while living in that house. Fortunately, she survived and is now in another facility. Whole life recovery is very unprofessional and does not provide any valuable treatment there. The staff at whole life lied to me on numerous occasions.[146]

Kigar and Hutson also negotiated illegal kickbacks with laboratories that tested patient urine. Just as Kigar disguised referral payments as "case management" services, the kickbacks from labs were called "investment dividends."[147]

At this point, the fledgling Sober Homes Task Force had still not made its first arrest. That changed in October 2016 when Aronberg, Padich, and Johnson decided the evidence was enough to put handcuffs around the wrists of Kigar and Hutson. Because of legal challenges and then COVID delays, Kigar's trial would be delayed until August 2021. By then, prosecutors had filed 119 felony counts of patient brokering against the Whole Life CEO.

In 2017, the Sober Homes Task Force was investigating a drug testing business named Coastal Laboratory—which had billed insurance companies more than $141 million—when James

Kigar's name came up again. The investigation revealed that Kigar's Whole Life Recovery received kickbacks of $5,401.40 in exchange for sending patient urine to the Coastal lab. On March 18, 2019, Padich submitted another probable cause affidavit for Kigar's arrest on these two separate charges of patient brokering, and he was taken back into custody. Two weeks later, Kigar pleaded guilty to the new charges and was sentenced to three years of probation. Since the total kickback amount was small and his guilty plea was quick, Kigar was able to avoid incarceration. His trial on the other 119 felony counts, however, lay ahead.[148]

Hutson, meanwhile, chose to plead guilty in exchange for an eighteen-month prison term, but fled to Spain on the day he was required to turn himself in. To this day, he remains a fugitive from justice.[149]

At Kigar's trial, Assistant State Attorney Justin Chapman waved the Whole Life's "case management" forms in front of the jury, using the acronym "CYA" ("cover your ass") to proclaim them a bogus cover to protect against patient brokering charges. Using the forms as a prop, Chapman turned Kigar's best defense into a liability, telling the jury that "these forms were useless. They documented nothing and did nothing to help patients. That's because they were not meant for the patients. They were meant for you! They were meant to fool you!"

By contrast, Kigar's defense portrayed the yoga instructor as a well-meaning neophyte, an unsophisticated rube who was in over his head. To illustrate this point, defense counsel pointed out that Whole Life Recovery operated in the red. Taking the stand in his own defense, Kigar testified he was unfamiliar with the law, and he never made money from the treatment center after paying expenses, including those "case management" fees. Kigar said that he and his patients were shocked and scared when investigators from the Sober Homes Task Force showed up at the facility's door one day in police gear with guns drawn. He said that his vulnerable patients scattered at the show of force. Kigar's attorney followed by asking if it was true that some patients never returned for their much-needed treatment after the trauma of the Task Force's actions. Kigar replied in the affirmative, which elicited a final question before the weekend break: "How many of those patients overdosed and died that day because they didn't get the treatment they needed?"

At that moment, Justin Chapman successfully objected to the inflammatory and irrelevant question. But the damage was done. The question lingered in the juror's minds all weekend, with the implication that no matter how Whole Life operated, government intervention made things worse.

Although ignorance of the law is not an excuse for patient brokering charges, Kigar's attorneys skillfully combined it with a "no harm, no foul" defense to appeal to the jury's compassion and humanity. It only helped the defense's pitch that Kigar faced 119 charges—enough to imprison the supposedly sincere simpleton for the rest of his life.

As jury deliberations stretched into a third day, it was clear the defense approach was having an impact. In criminal trials, the judge instructs the jury to follow the law and base a verdict solely on the evidence, not sympathy, passion, or personal sentiments. But jury nullification, where jurors disregard the instructions and set a defendant free, occasionally happens. It's always a prosecutor's nightmare, and it occurred here.

In the first, and to this day, only "not guilty" verdict since the creation of the Sober Homes Task Force, a Palm Beach County jury acquitted James Kigar of all 119 counts against him. To add insult to injury, prosecutor Justin Chapman had to sit stoically while the jury foreperson repeated each charge, followed by the painful two-word verdict 119 separate times. Comparing it to the destructive power of horcruxes in the Harry Potter series, Chapman lamented that "a small piece of my soul died every time I heard another 'not guilty.'"

In a statement, a victorious Kigar said, "I applaud the efforts of all who seek to eliminate the dishonesty in the industry, however had [prosecutors] been more thorough in their assessment of my character and integrity, the misunderstanding and my arrest would not have occurred."[150]

Kigar's wife, Kelly Wick Kigar, was not as charitable towards the Task Force. In a Facebook post right after the verdict, she wrote:

> *What happens when your life is disrupted by lies, accusations and overreaching prosecution . . . for almost five years? You breathe and you put faith in God, the universe, whatever it is you believe in, then you breathe some more. You place faith in the jury, despite not being able to tell the whole story, that they see the truth. With your hands tied behind your back and weights on your ankles you run headfirst into a burning building, and you pray.*

Chapman and Johnson, meanwhile, attributed the defeat to jury nullification, but also second-guessed a few of their own trial decisions. The number one regret? Charging Kigar with 119 counts. Chapman described it as the biggest mistake of his career. But the law at the time may have forced Chapman's hand. Before the Sober Homes Task Force convinced the Florida legislature to change the law in 2017, patient brokering remained a third-degree felony punishable by up to five years in prison for each count—although sentencing guidelines made anything close to the maximum unrealistic except for career criminals. Before the legislative changes, a third-degree felony was the maximum charge, regardless of whether a defendant committed patient brokering once or a thousand times. After the 2017 amendments, however, patient brokering involving between ten and nineteen patients is now a second-degree felony punishable by up to fifteen years in prison. Patient brokering involving twenty or more patients is a first-degree felony punishable by up to thirty years in prison. If the new law had applied to Kigar, he could have been charged with one first-degree felony count, instead of 119 third-degree felonies.[151]

Johnson, the top prosecutor on the Sober Homes Task Force, explained that patient brokering trials can be challenging in front of a jury. "You don't usually have a clear-cut, sympathetic victim as you do in a robbery, homicide, or elder abuse case," said Johnson. "With drug treatment scams, you often have willing victims who are receiving illegal benefits, so they don't have a lot of jury appeal," said Johnson. "There may not even be victim testimony at all. At the same time, the jury sees a defendant who claims a pure heart and benevolent motivations."[152]

Johnson surmised that in the Kigar case, "the jury felt sorry for him. He was a terrible businessman by his own admission, a yoga instructor who got into the industry and never made money. He testified, and the jury gave him a pass, a jury pardon, rather than launch him with 119 counts."

The day after the verdict, the Sober Homes Task Force received a phone call they did not expect. It was Christopher Hutson. Now that Kigar was acquitted, Hutson offered to come back to Palm Beach County in exchange for a sweetheart deal. When Hutson bolted to Spain, he lost his eighteen-month plea bargain, as the judge instead imposed a five-year prison sentence. Still sore from losing the Kigar case, Chapman took some solace in quickly rejecting Hutson's opportunistic offer. Although Palm Beach County is unable to extradite someone from Spain for a third-degree felony, the warrant for Hutson's arrest remains active. Knowing that Hutson's family, including his daughter, still lives locally, Chapman insists it is just a matter of time until Hutson returns to the United States and faces justice.

When prosecutors file criminal charges, they must have a good faith basis to believe that they can get a conviction beyond a reasonable doubt. Even the most confident prosecutors know there are no sure things, as the only predictable thing about juries is that they are notoriously unpredictable. Although it is obviously disappointing to lose a case, it is preferable to never being able to develop enough evidence to pursue charges in the first place. One of the worst parts of a prosecutor's job is to tell victims of crime and their desperate families that an offender cannot be found or cannot be brought to justice. These are the cases that torment Padich and his team. They continue to motivate them to keep their foot on the gas pedal.

CHAPTER 8

PARADISE LOST

Before she was old enough to attend kindergarten, Jenna Jacobsen enjoyed her early childhood on Long Island without a care in the world. She and her friends frequently rode their bikes and scooters through the neighborhood, or went swimming in the nearby lake, under the watchful eye of their parents, or with Jenna's older sister as an unofficial third parent. When Dr. Dave Campbell interviewed Jenna's father, Chris, by telephone several times in March of 2020, Chris said that even as a young child, Jenna could sense something wrong with the relationship between him and her mother.[153] How could she not? They were always fighting. His wife had a drinking problem, and eventually Jenna recognized that as well. Her mom often slurred her words and fell asleep on the couch in the middle of the day.

Jenna was only five years old when her parents divorced, which led her father to move out of town for work. He missed large swathes of his children's early development yet did his best to rekindle the relationships with his children after reuniting with them a few years after the divorce.

Jenna was fifteen, still living at home with her alcohol-im-paired mother, when her older sister called Chris to say that drugs were found in Jenna's room. Chris thought he was a dil-igent and observant father but was blindsided by this shocking news about his youngest daughter. He told Campbell that she had never demonstrated any mental health or substance use issues, although he later learned that Jenna had started taking prescription opioid pain pills, given to her years before by her mother for a toothache. That was when life began to unravel for the teenager.

Chris had not visited the house where his daughters lived with their mother for quite a while, but the terrible news about the drugs prompted him to stop by. He was appalled by the living conditions. According to Chris, "the place was a wreck, trashed, horrible." He said that he really lost it. He went through his daughter's bedroom and found even more drugs stashed away, prescription opioids and other substances he did not recognize. He even learned during that visit that Jenna's boyfriend had re-cently died of a drug overdose in that very same room. Besides the feeling of loss his daughter was contending with, Chris was beside himself with grief, intermixed with boiling anger and a gnawing pit of anxiety in his stomach.

"Get your stuff," Chris ordered. "You're coming home and staying with me from now on." Jenna tried to put up a fuss, but in the end, gathered her personal belongings and left with her father. Predictably, once living in his home, the transition to structured living under the watchful eye of her father did not go well. The domestic rancor that raged between a father intent on stopping his daughter's drug use, and the compulsions and cravings of her addiction, were too much for them. As Chris recalled, it was not long before Jenna agreed to enter a local inpatient detox treatment program. It would be her first, but not last stint in rehab.

The years between Jenna's sixteenth and twentieth birthdays were a struggle. She and her father butted heads at every turn. Living her formative years in a loosely supervised home taught her she could lie, cheat, and manipulate with impunity. Chris spent those years trying to break Jenna of those old habits and teach her coping skills, to no avail. Jenna could not durably recover from opioid addiction despite professional and family support. Each attempt to guide her through successful recovery eventually failed with relapse, until finally, as she neared the age of twenty, there was mounting optimism that she would make it.

"Half of Jenna's friends have died of overdose," Chris told Campbell. "I would say more than half died of fentanyl overdose." With her father's commitment to structure, discipline, and unconditional love, Jenna achieved an apparent lasting recovery near her twentieth birthday. She had her own bank account, a steady job at a local supermarket, and dreamed of a career in veterinary medicine. She was still living with her father, and the bright smile she had in her younger years again covered her face in a warm glow. Jenna and her father were building a foundation of trust one day at a time. Chris started teaching his daughter how to drive the family car and was planning to buy her a used car of her own. They both agreed that he would help her rent a small apartment in Long Island so she could begin living independently. Sitting around the dinner table in the evening, Chris and Jenna were even talking about the day when she would go off to college and study to become a veterinarian, as caring for animals was her passion and calling. Thriving in life and maintaining a stable recovery, the toxic mist of addiction was becoming less perceptible month after month, like a fog bank lifting off the Long Island coast.

Chris remembered the winter of 2019 because it was snowing like crazy in New York. His job driving the big snowplow trucks for the Highway Department deployed him upstate for a few days. Canada had over three feet of snow and the roads near the border were in desperate need of clearing. Out-of-town and overtime pay were good money that he and Jenna could really use. After the blizzard had passed and the roads had cleared, Chris headed home, bleary-eyed and sore. He arrived on a Friday by dinnertime, where he found that Jenna had tidied up the place. He noticed Jenna's ebullient smile, which helped lift his own spirits. As he was heading to the shower to wash away the road grime, something on the kitchen table caught his eye. He took a closer look and his mood instantly darkened. Jenna had left drug paraphernalia in plain view on the table. Chris knew her drug use was serious when he recognized burned foil and a lighter to allow Jenna to inhale smoke from an illicit substance. While he did not know what drug she had used, it was no wonder she was smiling brightly: she was high. Jenna had relapsed—again.

Chris exclaimed, "What the hell is this?!" His anger made Jenna recoil. Chris had thought everything was going so well, but now his world was crashing down. His daughter's elevated mood came to a grinding halt. She started crying and said she did not even know why she used drugs again. Tragically, she told her father she was simply bored while he was out of town, feeling a bit down, and wanted a pick-me-up. The cravings of opioid addiction were too much for her to withstand in an empty house in the dark dead of winter, with ice and snow blanketing the frozen ground outside.

"Jenna, we've been here before," Chris said. "You know there is zero tolerance in my household." She knew the rules of her father's house and knew she had to go, so she quickly packed a bag and walked out the front door to stay with a friend. Neither Chris nor Jenna offered goodbyes or apologies that night, and Chris did not hear from his daughter again for two days, when she called from a detox center located on Long Island. For Jenna's father, this is where the real nightmare began.

Jenna had already cycled through several stints in detox and rehab, including once before at a facility near their home in East Islip. Jenna was an adult and able to check herself in. She was covered through her father's health insurance. A swipe of the credit card, confirmation of the validity of her health insurance, and bingo, she was admitted. Although Chris was pleased with his daughter's initiative, and told her so, he did not like the staff at this detox center and had a deep-seated, gnawing anxiety about this relapse. Something was different and ominous this time, yet he could not put a finger on it.

"I don't even want to do this anymore," Jenna told her father over the telephone. She was so happy when Chris told her how proud he was of her. "We will take it from here and start over again," he told her. Unconditional love flowed from every nook and cranny in her father's heart and mind.

Chris reaffirmed his strong belief that she should not leave Long Island after completing the several-day detox program. He also let her know that his home would always remain her home.

If Jenna felt it was better for her recovery to spend a month in an inpatient drug rehabilitation program, Chris said he would help with the arrangements. All the while, he implored Jenna to stay in Long Island because of concerns for her safety. He had been hearing horror stories about sober houses in Florida that were in cahoots with shady detox and rehab centers. Although Jenna promised her father that she would stay local, Chris knew Jenna's word could not be trusted as long as she was under the opioid spell.

A salt-of-the-earth, blue-collar worker devoted to his daughter, Chris understood some of the challenges facing Jenna. He was twenty years into his own recovery from alcohol addiction and recognized the importance of having a support network nearby. Social connectedness is critical for mental health, including the resilience needed to recover from drug addiction.

Chris had a gut feeling that the counselors at the center's detox program were not trustworthy. He called and confronted a supervisor. Chris admitted to Campbell that he could be harsh in his words at times. "If you send my kid off Long Island," Chris said to the supervisor, "we're going to have problems, me and you."

Even with this latest relapse, Chris still felt a growing bond of trust with Jenna. He was becoming more comfortable with her decision-making capabilities than he had been in years. She was a more mature adult and had been getting her act together. Even so, he had a nagging suspicion that her latest relapse had been going on for a while. He did not, however, have any faith in the detox center, or the counselor on the phone who told him that she was twenty years old and capable of making her own decisions.

"No, she's not!" Chris replied. "Yeah, she might be a twenty-year-old, but you're talking about a child who's coming down from an opioid addiction. And not just with Jenna, that's true for all addicted kids in her age group." Chris knew from experience that five days of being in a detox center, after weeks, months, or even years of drug use, does not qualify the patient to make any life-changing decisions. "These kids put their trust in these detox counselors to guide them in the right direction," Chris asserted. "But in my experience, these frickin' detox counselors are in this patient body broker business. The counselors put the kids up for bid." He explained that the price for the patient's stay in drug rehab depended upon the quality of the patient's insurance. Chris had concerns about drug rehab centers in general, whether in New York or elsewhere, that were intent on shuffling kids down to Florida.

"You get these kids up here in the Northeast admitted into these detox centers," Chris said. "Then they are put up on the black market and the bidding starts, like the slave trade in the United States hundreds of years ago. The kids go to the highest bidder to stay in rehab housing down in South Florida or other places."

Chris described the system as an organized bidding process on the internet. "The counselors show these ignorant, naïve kids pretty pictures of palm trees and frickin' jet-skis or horseback riding, and all types of meditation, massages, acupuncture and other stuff," he said. "The kids are thinking, wow, I could go down there to recover—sign me up! When they finally get off the plane and into the actual rehab housing, they're shitholes, literally!"

Chris's research and personal experience taught him how well-intended federal laws enable the chicanery in the Florida Shuffle. "The parents know nothing about it because these so-called counselors and scam rehabs are hiding behind all the HIPAA laws and confidentiality acts," he told Dr. Campbell. "So once your kid goes into a detox, you don't know what happens to them. They are over eighteen years old. They don't tell you anything. The kids disappear and then they pop up in a rehab somewhere or something. If the parent is lucky, the center calls them."

After Chris's blowup with the detox supervisor, it was the last time he heard from that center. Against his wishes, the facility transferred Jenna to a treatment center in New Jersey. Even though Jenna was enrolled in the family plan under his employer-supported health insurance, Chris had no say whatsoever in the matter. She left the relative security of Long Island, where her father was a short drive away, to "a real shady rehab facility in South Jersey," according to Chris.

Jenna completed several weeks of drug rehabilitation. When Campbell asked Chris for more information, he said that Jenna had cycled so many times through rehab programs that he lost track of some of the details. On this occasion, when Jenna came home again for the umpteenth time, Chris reiterated his position to her that leaving Long Island was not an idea he supported. She promised not to do that again, which was yet another promise soon to be broken. "Okay, daddy," she said. "I'll stay here."

Jenna maintained her recovery for almost a year. She lived under her father's roof and abided by his rules the entire time. Chris and Jenna's older sister heaped praise, love, understanding, and encouragement on her. Jenna was excited to be so close to living on her own in an apartment she rented for herself, owning a car, getting into school again. Becoming a veterinarian was never far from her mind.

"I'm doing this on my own now," she told her father. "I'm going to get better."

Relapse, however, happens all too often with opioid addiction, whether it's pain pills, heroin, or fentanyl. When polypharmacy is mixed into the equation, as is common with cocaine or methamphetamine, recovery is exquisitely fragile. Jenna started using again and returned to the same treatment center in South Jersey. She met a guy at the rehab and the two of them soon moved to what Chris called "scam-type rehab housing" in Red Banks, New Jersey. It was her new boyfriend's old stomping grounds. His buddies still lived there, which was a recipe for relapse. The minute she left rehab, Jenna was using drugs again, and this time, living in a cheap motel, better known as a flophouse. Chris never learned the name of that boyfriend.

Jenna's habit of lying, cheating, and manipulating her father was as predictable as the sunrise. After several more weeks, she called her father and said, "This is crazy. I just want to come home." But first, Jenna said she wanted to get herself straightened out, which was her shorthand for easing into recovery. She checked herself into detox once again, this time at a center in Toms River, New Jersey. After being admitted and settled into her room, Jenna called her father to ask for money—a red flag for Chris. Every time she asked for cash, he would eventually learn that she used it on drugs, whether in detox, rehab, at home, or out on her own. Like so many others, once Jenna was using again, deceit, gaming the system and manipulative behaviors were the calling cards. Chris maintains that she learned these characteristics from years living with a mother who suffered from severe alcohol use disorder.

At the detox center in Tom's River, Jenna met a new boyfriend, "Teddy," and the two fled the facility to get high in a nearby motel. Teddy, who had been through multiple cycles of relapse, was a veteran of the Florida Shuffle. He convinced Jenna to travel together to the Sunshine State, explaining that a treatment center in Coral Springs would send them free plane tickets in exchange for entering their inpatient facility. Even better, Teddy insisted, the treatment center would admit them as a couple.

Such an arrangement obviously creates negative consequences with a harmful impact on recovery. It is never easy to get past the intense cravings of addiction that can lead to relapse. Living with a boyfriend or girlfriend who also has a substance use disorder makes the stakes even higher, and the odds of maintaining a durable recovery even lower. Unethical treatment centers, however, are motivated by closing the deal with a patient who has generous insurance coverage rather than concentrating on sound treatment protocols and putting the patient's health first. Teddy lacked health insurance coverage, so the deal he brokered with the Florida rehab center was dependent upon getting Jenna, with her father's excellent insurance, into treatment with him.

Jenna's father had no idea of the whereabouts of his daughter until he received her call from Florida. He asked her where she was, to which she responded, "In South Florida, in Coral Springs." Chris was flabbergasted and said, "Oh, my God, are you kidding me? How the hell did you get there?"

"Oh, we flew down," she said. She then asked for money. Chris knew to decline her request and offered instead to go down there and get her. That conversation, like so many in the past, ended quickly after he refused Jenna's request for cash. What made that conversation most memorable was that the next words were the last he would ever hear from his daughter.

"They're taking the phone away," she said to her father. "I got to go. They're taking the phone away." The phone clicked and was silent. Chris held on for much longer than normal, listening to the silence, with a vague sense of foreboding.

Chris learned that Jenna and Teddy had been in the Edge Recovery Center in Coral Springs, but decided, for reasons that he never learned, to travel north to a different recovery center in Palm Beach County. On Thursday, April 25, 2019, the couple headed up to the new rehab. Chris told Campbell that he was not sure about their means of transportation, but he did recall receiving a phone call that night around seven o'clock from a representative of the center in Palm Beach County.

The rep told Chris that his daughter had just called and wanted them to send a car to pick her up "in the Lantana or Lake Worth area at some location." The caller needed to verify coverage from the health insurance policyholder before he could send a car out to get her. Red flags instantly popped up in Chris's mind. When it came to the health and safety of his youngest daughter, Chris was never one to mince words and proceeded to interrogate the rep on the phone.

"I'm getting wind of all this insurance fraud that's been going on with all these so-called rehab facilities," Chris said to the rep. "Who the hell are you? What kind of credentials do you have?

Is this for a reputable place or just another one of these scam places?"

After just a couple of minutes into the conversation, Chris knew something was terribly wrong. He knew his daughter was in real trouble this time. The nightmare was intensifying with each passing moment. He was desperate and convinced that he needed to take immediate action to protect Jenna. Chris just needed to decide what the next step was: Was she going to West Palm Beach or somewhere else? And why couldn't he get a straight answer from anyone?

The rehab facility must have thought Jenna's health insurance coverage checked out, because the facility dispatched a car to pick up the couple. Meanwhile, Jenna and Teddy were idly waiting at the pickup location in Central Palm Beach County when a vigilant police officer stopped his cruiser and got out to question them. He found that Teddy had a felony warrant back in New York and had violated his probation by traveling to Florida. The situation quickly went from bad to worse when Jenna's new boyfriend lost his cool and tried to strike the police officer and take off. It is never a good thing when a probation violator tries to commit a battery on a law enforcement officer and then outrun him, but addicts are often known to act in incomprehensible ways.

Much to Teddy's chagrin, the physically fit police officer ran a lot faster than a drug-addled, cigarette smoking, sedentary young man. The police officer pulled his taser and gave Teddy a jolt, followed by a pair of handcuffs. He was going to top off Teddy's experience with law enforcement by giving him a ride to the local police station in the back of his police cruiser.

Once the sweaty officer returned to the young woman, she was nowhere to be found. By the time the driver from the drug rehab facility arrived at the pickup location, both prospective patients were gone. Jenna had disappeared into the neighborhood, and Teddy had been arrested and was on his way to jail.

Teddy called his mother from jail, which led to a call to Chris that his daughter had disappeared. Chris raced to pack a bag, but before he could leave for Florida, the rehab center rep called him again. Chris asked if they had his daughter and was told no, she wasn't there. The driver had hung out for a little bit, looked around, could not find anyone, and then returned to the facility.

Chris hung up and immediately called the Palm Beach County Sheriff's Office (PBSO). He sent them several photos of Jenna and booked a flight to Florida. Never one to rely on others when it came to his family, Chris decided to find his daughter by himself, whether he got help from law enforcement or not. He knew time was of the essence in searching for Jenna, so he reached out by phone to local media in the Palm Beach area. He also found the number on the internet for Palm Beach County's Sober Homes Task Force and gave them a call. Aronberg remembers how his Task Force investigators hit the streets and knocked on doors in the search for clues as soon as they received the phone call from Chris, who was still in New York.

A law enforcement official suggested to Chris that he check with his health insurance company for any suspicious activity, but that recommendation fell flat when Chris called a company representative and was stonewalled. The health insurance carrier refused to give him any information because of HIPAA patient confidentiality laws. The representative said that because Jenna was an adult, Chris was not authorized to access her healthcare information, even though she was insured under his group policy. It did not matter that she was missing and the subject of a police search.

Chris felt like he was sitting in purgatory, receiving words of support and encouragement from all corners, yet blocked by patient protection laws not flexible enough to accommodate the individual circumstances of his daughter's disappearance. About five days after Jenna's disappearance in the Lantana/Lake Worth area of Palm Beach County, the desperate father made his way to the airport. Although it is fewer than three hours by plane, Chris's trip to the Sunshine State felt like it took forever. The anxiety swirling in his gut and grinding in his mind was like acid mixed with nails. Images of Jenna riding her bike as a child with her hair blowing in the breeze, smiling, laughing, having fun—it formed a collage that he could not shake. The red mist of rage made his blood boil and his heart race. He was torn between anger and anguish combined with a deep, unbidden sense of dread.

CHAPTER 9

BOTTOMING OUT

The aircraft touched down at Palm Beach International Airport with a jolt. Palm trees nestled along the roadway adjacent to the airport waved their fronds in a futile attempt to beckon the focused father to enjoy a tropical vacation. Chris was having none of that. He grabbed his carry-on and scrambled out the door and off the tarmac with one mission in mind: Find Jenna.

Chris wasted no time. He rented a cheap car and immediately began scouring the streets for clues. Even before getting a room at a nearby motel, Chris drove to the area where his daughter was last seen. Hours turned into days as he expanded his search. He constantly drove and walked through neighborhoods and city streets, stopping to speak to anyone who would listen. He only paused for a catnap now and then. He spent days and nights on the streets, a stranger in a strange land, with the occasional detour into the offices of local officials. Chris could not sleep, so he was rarely in his motel room.

When Chris encountered people in his search, he would hold up Jenna's picture and talk to them about her disappearance. He would ask: "Have you seen this girl?" At times, he was pleading. One or two said yes, some said no, and many others looked at him with passive indifference.

Aronberg and his team members had a five-day head start on Chris. While Chris worked his telephone in New York, the Sober Homes Task Force personnel questioned their sources and made new ones. They searched day and night for the missing New Yorker, following leads and investigating clues to learn her whereabouts. By the time Jenna's father arrived in Palm Beach County, the team members had made no progress. It was like she had disappeared into thin air.

Days turned into weeks without any news about Jenna's whereabouts. Aronberg's team of seasoned law enforcement officials feared the worst. Chris was beside himself with grief, but never gave up. He was tough, fearless, and committed to finding his daughter alive.

Chris remembered his first face-to-face meeting with Palm Beach County detectives in what he called "a soulless PBSO conference room," feeling frustrated and desperate. He had not slept in days since flying to Florida and was getting nowhere fast in his frantic search. He asked the detectives to tell him about their efforts. They stared back at him in silence. One of the detectives gave Chris a little piece of paper with "a couple of scratches marked on it with some street names and a location."

"This is it?" Chris asked. "Is this all you have?"

From that point forward, the meeting in the Sheriff's office went from bad to worse. Chris, in his own words, "fucking freaked out on them." No sleep, but plenty of anxiety, agitation, and a missing daughter. It all came out. But freaking out on law enforcement, in their own office, or anywhere for that matter, is usually a bad idea. After a few more choice words that Chris tried to forget, he turned and stormed out of the PBSO building. His hands were shaking as he clutched the piece of paper in a death grip. He does not remember the drive back to his motel. It was all a blur of adrenaline and anger. He knew he had created a rift that could impede further efforts to find his daughter through PBSO, so he changed gears. Chris swung by the motel office and grabbed a piping hot cup of terrible-tasting coffee. Then he went to his room and got on the phone. Chris had a growing concern that Jenna could be a victim of human trafficking because of what he read on the internet. He had learned that young women were particularly vulnerable to being victims of modern-day slavery, especially those with a substance use disorder. It only took a few calls and he was connected with a high-powered local advocacy group, the Human Trafficking Coalition of the Palm Beaches. He thought, *now I am getting somewhere.*

A day or two later—Chris could not remember how long it was—he sat in a fifty-foot circle of well-dressed community leaders at one of the coalition group's meetings. He told Campbell later that he felt woefully out of place in that room full of people, seeing himself as an old, distraught, blue-collar dad surrounded by expensive suits, ties, and dresses. Chris was introduced to the group and told the story of his daughter's disappearance only days before. Those in attendance embraced Chris with love and compassion. Some in the room told Chris the same thing had happened to their son or daughter. Chris's daughter was not the first victim of what he learned was called the Florida Shuffle.

Chris had already reached out to the local television stations and newspapers. Once in town, he turned up the heat. The media is always looking for a story, and they were eager to report on Jenna's disappearance and the search. Chris did not stop there. He asked the community for help. He met so many strangers in those early days and weeks that he lost track of some of their names. Many community members, as well as the Sober Homes Task Force, rallied to Chris's side.

It only took a few days for Chris to realize some of the streets in Palm Beach County were not safe for him to walk through, especially in the dark of night. He told Campbell that some neighborhoods in Central Palm Beach County looked like a war zone to him.

"When I wandered a few streets off Federal Highway," he said. "It was just one motel after another, and they're heavily guarded, heavily armed, and you just don't go in there. Drugs and prostitution, you name it. These kids from up north come down to these scam rehabs, and these places let them cohabitate with each other. There's minimal, if any, treatment. They house them with no restrictions and no supervision, nothing. The only rule is the residents must be in by 11:00 p.m. So, what they are doing is bilking the insurance companies for millions of dollars."

Chris was convinced Jenna was targeted because she was afflicted by the brain disease of addiction and had good health insurance to pay for treatment. He learned during his search, from talking to others who had lost family members to the system, that Jenna was victimized by the patient body brokering system that was foundational in the Florida Shuffle. "They kept her sick, using, hooked on drugs," he said. "She realized, because she was a smart kid, this was bullshit. She wanted to get better and come home. It's my belief she thought she was heading up to Palm Beach County to get into a more legit place. But when she left her New Jersey rehab for Florida, it was due to the Florida Shuffle, plain and simple."

Fearless and ever-more determined, Chris walked the dangerous alleys and street corners of Palm Beach County's drug underworld. He later recalled telling a local newspaper that he "saw Jenna" in the faces of others "every day and every night."

Chris speculated, from the information he learned during his search for Jenna, that once the police left the scene and took Teddy to jail, she was literally grabbed off the street in an attempt to force her into human trafficking. He believes that she must have vigorously resisted and was beaten in the process. Chris said that Jenna was raised to be tough, proud, and unafraid to fight back.

"I was looking for my daughter nonstop for weeks, walking the streets, and handing out flyers made with Jenna's photo," Chris said. "Crime Stoppers were on it too. I hit every freaking store. It got to the point where all the dealers sitting all day on the bench at the bus stop selling drugs in front of Walgreens knew who I was, and what I was doing. There was this one drug dealer, casual as hell, always munching on some fries and waiting for the next customer to roll up and buy some dope. We used to talk and stuff, and he'd be like: 'Yo, Dad.' They were calling me 'Dad' down there. 'Did you find your daughter yet?' I'm like: 'No, you're supposed to be helping me.' The young dealer would just laugh and go right back to selling drugs."

Chris spent a solid month searching for Jenna. On the last day of his search, he was in his motel room sipping early morning coffee. He had hired an attorney and a private investigator and was mulling over where to look next. At about 10:00 a.m., the private investigator arrived to say that he could not find Jenna anywhere. The investigator told Chris this has only happened once or so in his entire career, and that he always finds the missing kids. "I just don't understand it," he mused. "The only thing I can think of is that they sold Jenna off to another group down in Hialeah or Miami, Delray, Orlando, or took her down to Haiti or even Europe." The seasoned investigator understood that human trafficking enterprises ran deep. He knew Palm Beach County was in the top three counties in Florida for human trafficking, in a state that was in the top three in the country.

The meeting ended, leaving Chris sitting by himself, nursing another cup of bad motel coffee. He thought, *I'm at a dead end. I don't know what else to do. We've done everything, and we can't find her.*

Suddenly, a bright light flashed in his mind. He had an epiphany and almost fell out of his chair. Cold coffee spilled on his lap as he thought: *I'm going to start hitting those motels, which everybody said to avoid. They told me they will kill you, but at this point I have no other choice. So, I'm going for it.*

Chris ran to his rental car, fired it up and raced to the beginning of a strip of cheap, dangerous, fleabag motels. He got lost on the way and wound up at a stop sign somewhere in the middle of Lake Worth. Out of the corner of his eye he saw an expensive Porsche fly by. He thought: *Wow, a Porsche. Really? In this part of town? You've got to be kidding.* The expensive import stuck out like a sore thumb in the sea of dented, rusty, and dirty sedans. Then, for no apparent reason, the flashy ride skidded to a stop, right in the middle of the road. Chris watched as a woman wriggled out of the Porsche, first one long leg and then the other. No sooner was she out of the car than she sashayed down the street, apparently looking for a john. The Porsche turned at the corner and parked as she crossed the street in front of Chris's car. He kept a watchful eye on her, wondering whether she might know something about Jenna. *What the heck,* he pulled up to her and held out the flyer with Jenna's photograph.

"Hey, how are you doing?" Chris asked.

"Hi," she replied through a tight-lipped smile that struggled to conceal decayed meth and tobacco-stained teeth. Chris could not help but think of Jenna's wide, toothy grin in her happier days.

He introduced himself as Chris Jacobsen and told her he had come down to Lake Worth from Long Island to look for his daughter, who was missing. The young woman took the flyer from Chris's hand without a word and burst into tears as she looked down at Jenna's face. The tears streamed down her cheeks and quickly smeared her thickly applied mascara. Chris's heart skipped a beat: *She knows something about my Jenna.* He opened his car door and got out, right in the middle of the street. Her crying caused Chris's eyes to well up with tears. They were quite a sight. It did not look like the typical sex worker-john interaction that was common in that part of town.

She told Chris she had not seen his daughter but had heard something. As she continued to sob, she asked "Is this why there's so many cops around? Are they lookin' for your daughter?"

"Absolutely, yes," Chris replied.

"Wow," was all she could say as she tried to catch her breath.

Chris looked at someone who at one time was an attractive young woman with hopes and dreams. She must have been in her twenties but looked sixty. There were scars up and down her arms, round holes that had long since scabbed over and healed with the telltale signs of skin-popping or intravenous drug use with abscesses. Her once-smooth skin was weathered like an old sailor who had spent too many days in the Caribbean sun and too many nights in the rum barrel. She looked beaten down, worn out, tattered, and pitiful. Chris felt deeply sorry for her. As they both stood in the middle of the street crying, he could not stop thinking about his own Jenna, and what she must be going through at that very moment.

He looked directly into the woman's soggy, swollen, and bloodshot eyes and asked what she had heard. She responded by shaking her head and said she just heard that she was missing, and her dad was looking for her, that's all. Disappointed at the lack of information but grateful for the woman's humanity, Chris told her she could get help and escape this death spiral.

She looked down at the ground, away from Jenna's photo emblazoned on the flyer, and told him that she couldn't get away. "I'm in too much, too deep, and I can't get out," she cried.

All Chris could muster to say was, "Oh my God."

She stopped sobbing enough to tell him that if she saw her or heard anything, she would call the numbers on the flyer. Chris thanked her and told her to take care of herself. He considered giving her a big hug, but thought better of it, given that he was standing conspicuously in the middle of the street. Instead, he slid into the rental car and dropped it into gear. As he started pulling away, Chris could not stop looking into his rearview mirror. The sight of the lost soul tore at his heart.

As Chris put his eyes back on the road in front of him, he caught a glimpse of a man climbing out of the parked Porsche and sprinting toward the young woman, who was still standing in the road. Chris spun around in his driver's seat and watched as the Porsche driver gesticulated angrily at her. Chris hit the brakes and the car skidded to a stop, still right in the middle of the street. *This guy's going to beat her down.* In the several weeks he had been canvassing the neighborhoods, Chris had already witnessed several violent assaults. They were all in the middle of the street. He assumed that pimps chose the public display to make an example of their victims, presumably prostitutes working under their control.

Fortunately, the interaction quickly cooled off after the young woman said a few words to him. They both kept glancing at Chris in the rental car. Then the pimp started frantically jumping up and down, waving his arms and calling to Chris, who quickly realized the man was trying to get him to come back. *Wow, what should I do? Should I go back? Is he going to shoot me?* It was in the middle of the day and his missing daughter's trail was starting to get cold. It had been weeks since he last spoke with her on the phone and the dozens of leads that he had received had all turned into dead ends.

Curious, scared, and desperate, Chris turned his car around. He could see that the woman had stopped crying. She had wiped the tears away with the back of her hand, smearing black mascara across her cheeks, which gave her a clownish appearance. The pimp had all the usual accoutrements of the trade, with a big gold chain draped around his neck, a gawdy, gold grill in his mouth, and tattoos adorning his arms and neck. Chris rolled up to the pimp and cracked open the window of his car, keeping one foot on the brake and the other on the accelerator just in case things went sideways.

The Porsche man spoke through the open window and said, "Yo, you're the dad, right?" Chris looked up at his face and replied in the affirmative. Porsche asked Chris if he was looking for his daughter, to which Chris nodded his head yes. He then told Chris his best friend lived nearby in John Prince Park, and asked Chris if he knew the area. Chris did. Porsche then told him that something went down the other night regarding his daughter. "What?" Chris asked timidly, fearing the worst. Porsche advised him to go to the park and find out for himself.

Chris's ears perked up even though he thought, *I've heard plenty of bullshit already.* He was skeptical and felt a setup was in the making.

"Really?" Chris asked again, this time emphatically. "Like what?"

"Yo, just go," the man said cryptically. "Look for him, short Puerto Rican dude with ink . . . like this." He showed Chris the tattoos up and down his gangly arms and neck. "Except he got ink all over his face too, and his hair is in pigtails."

"Alright, alright, I'm going," Chris replied as he slowly pulled away. Even as he eased down the road, he could see the pimp shooing him along, with a wave of his hands. He could see his lips saying: "Go-go." Chris wondered, *is this a setup or something? Are they trying to get me to the park to rip me off and kill me?*

Chris still had half a tank of gas as he turned onto Sixth Avenue heading toward John Prince Park. He kept his window rolled down to get some fresh air since the car's A/C was not working well enough to lower the temperature from swelter to simmer. He headed west and crossed the bridge over a canal connecting parts of the large freshwater lake within the park. Lake Osborne was rimmed by vegetation that was home to poisonous water moccasins and sharp-toothed alligators. More than once, an errant swimmer or water-skier has run afoul of these reptiles, with tragic results. After he crossed the bridge, Chris saw baseball, softball, and soccer fields teeming with kids in brightly colored uniforms, and large pavilions full of families enjoying the fresh air of the free county park.

He snapped out of the dream as he drove further, past the families, ball fields, and picnics until he was confronted by the grim reality of Tent City, the sprawling patchwork of makeshift roofs put together with assorted blue tarps, and even palmetto and palm fronds from the nearby woods. It was an enclave for the homeless living in a beautiful park in sunny South Florida. It was also very dangerous. In years past, the entire area was a safe and fun refuge. Not so anymore. Families now steered clear of it, and the only non-Tent City residents who dared enter the area were police officers.

Chris slowed down and held a flyer with Jenna's photo out the window as he pulled alongside a group of people gathered at the entrance to Tent City. All of them ominously turned to stare at him. He thought, *to hell with it,* and stopped to open his driver's side door. As he started to get out, he felt the sweat on his back glue his shirt onto his skin. As he stood, a tall, skinny woman separated from the crowd of gawking, glaring onlookers and came over to him.

"Hey, how you doin'?" she asked. It crossed Chris's mind that she thought he was a john looking for sex. He felt all eyes on him.

"You seen my daughter?" he asked. The apparent sex worker stared at Jenna's photo and started to gently cry, with tears welling up in her eyes and slowly rolling down her cheeks. She licked the salty tears from her lips without a word. *Twice in one day? Who would have thought?*

The silence finally broke when she whispered that she had not seen her. Chris thought her tears said otherwise.

All of a sudden, a man broke free from the crowd. He had tattoos on his face and arms, and pigtails like a pirate. He walked right up and put his face within a foot of Chris's. *Game on. This is going down right now.* He resisted the urge to turn and run, and instead asked Pigtails if he had seen his daughter, holding the flyer right in front of his nose. Chris's heart was pounding but he kept his hand from shaking though sheer willpower. To his disbelief, the rough-looking Pigtails started crying too. It was like a tear-fest in Palm Beach County that day. Chris dried his own eyes with the back of his other hand and felt a huge sigh of relief as he realized he was not going to get shot, knifed, or beaten.

"You know, I got a niña too," responded the pigtailed dude with a thick Puerto Rican accent that Chris recognized from some of his coworkers. He knew he had found the man he was looking for. Pigtails told Chris there was a big altercation in Tent City not too long ago over his daughter. Chris's heart began to race again. This was the first time he had come across someone with direct knowledge of Jenna's whereabouts. *Please tell me where she is, so I can hug her again*, he thought.

"There is this kingpin that runs Tent City and keeps the peace in the area," Pigtails said. "He came in here with a friend and they got a hold of this particular dude they called OG Red. They went over and beat this guy to near death. They were yelling at him as they beat him to the ground, that the girl OG Red murdered is the one everybody's looking for. They beat OG Red down so bad they almost killed him."

Chris's heart sank: *Murdered? The one everyone is looking for. Is that Jenna?* The question kept ricocheting in his mind, like it was bouncing off the inside of his thick skull. *My little girl may have been murdered.*

"So right away I lost it, and I backed off," Chris recounted. "I called the detectives with my cell, and they hightailed it to the park."

When the detectives appeared minutes later, Chris told them that Pigtails had described the murder of a girl that may have been Jenna. The detectives gave each other a knowing glance, as if the writing was on the wall. The four of them marched into Tent City, which scattered the squatters like a flock of birds escaping a predator.

"There were a thousand freaking pairs of eyes burning me up," Chris said. "I saw Pigtails and waved to him real friendly like. Others were scurrying away at the sight of the police, but not Pigtails. He held his ground."

Once up close, Chris whispered into Pigtails ear, "Listen, I'm sorry I got to bring the detectives in, but I got to find my kid."

"Everybody was very upset," Chris recalled. The detectives insisted that Pigtails give a statement and then made him sign it. Just as Chris and the detectives were starting to leave, Pigtails dropped a bomb. He told the detectives to go around the corner because there was something going on. He was trying to be secretive, speaking in hushed tones with what felt like a thousand eyes staring at them from behind the saw palmettos and oak trees. Pigtails knew that snitches had a short life span in Tent City, but he also did not want to be charged for playing any role in a murder.

They walked around the corner to where Pigtails had directed them and sure enough, the kingpin was sitting in a lawn chair with his muscular arms resting on a folding table like a monarch holding court. He was away from the throngs of homeless residents, perched underneath the relative comfort of a bright blue canvas canopy to block the scorching sun. Chris remembered the giant mosquitoes reveling in the unrelenting humidity as he and the detectives slowly approached. Kingpin's back and neck were ramrod straight. His eyes were covered with dark sunglasses. Not a single facial muscle contracted as the group of detectives and one pale northerner approached. Were it not for the circumstances, Kingpin might have been mistaken for a father keeping an eye on his children as they frolicked in the park. Chris knew better, though, surmising that Kingpin was the leader of a gang or criminal enterprise integrated into Tent City.

Chris slowly walked up and placed the flyer with Jenna's photo flat on the table in front of Kingpin. After a lengthy, tense silence, Chris softly asked if he knew anything about her. He muttered Jenna's name to Kingpin, almost as an afterthought.

Kingpin stared back with a deadpan gaze. Strangely, he never even glanced at the detectives who were standing behind Chris. Chris asked him a few more questions about Jenna but got nothing except an eerie silence. Chris, a bit of a self-admitted hothead, started to ratchet up the intensity of the questioning, getting louder and more hostile by the moment. Just as he reached a feverish and dangerous pitch, one of the detectives came up behind Chris and slowly pulled him away. After that detective handed Chris off to the other two, the detective walked back to Kingpin and had a chat with him out of earshot. Chris and the two remaining detectives had already walked backwards away from the blue canopy, remaining on high alert for any signs of danger. "Watch your six," one of the detectives said to Chris.

The detective who had hung back with Kingpin joined up with the group after only a minute or so. The foursome then eased out of Tent City on foot, jumped in their vehicles and drove out of the park. Once near the highway, the caravan pulled over to the side of the road where the group huddled around Chris's rental car. The detective who had pulled the hostile father away said that he could not believe what Chris had just done. He asked Chris if he knew who he was talking to in the park, and if he had a death wish.

"I was just screaming, hysterically screaming," Chris told Campbell. "I had lost complete control of my emotions because I knew what had happened." The detective that had hung back confirmed his worst suspicions, telling Chris that he believed Jenna had been murdered. The detective also said that Chris now had a contract on his head. "They wanted to kill me too," Chris recounted. "I was told they knew who I was, where I was staying, where I lived, and what I was doing down there." The detective told Chris that if that group ever saw him again, they would kill him on the spot. Chris was instructed to return to his motel and remain there while law enforcement did its job.

"Within twenty-four hours, the case went to homicide," Chris said. "After another day, I was told they found a body in a nature preserve in Lantana, and that it might be my daughter. They didn't know yet. One of the detectives told me that there was a forensic crime team at the scene, including an anthropologist—all types of people who investigate a murder."

"The remains were in such bad shape they requested me to get dental records," Chris said. "So, I got dental records. That's what it took to positively ID her. They had to fly somebody down from Washington, DC to verify and to confirm that those remains were Jenna."

"That was May 30th, 2019," Chris said. "That's the day I knew for sure that my daughter was dead."

Five weeks after Jenna had disappeared, her bones were found in a scrub area in Lantana, only a couple of miles from where she ran away as Teddy unsuccessfully resisted arrest. Aronberg's investigators believe that Jenna's murderer picked her up soon after she fled the scene. To this day, police continue to investigate her death as a homicide but have made no arrests.

As for Jenna's boyfriend, Teddy, who led the couple to Florida to reap the illicit benefits of the Florida Shuffle, his legal woes continued. Law enforcement found out that he had arrest warrants and probation violations back in New Jersey, so he was extradited to face charges back home after serving time in the Palm Beach County jail.

"Based on everything I know," Chris lamented, "Jenna was abducted off the street, brutally beaten and raped, and then murdered. I know the killer or killers tore her body apart and then buried her in a nature preserve. When wild animals found her body, they dug her up from the hole and ate her remains, scattering her bones around the area. That picture is what I have in my head every fucking night going to bed."

Chris soon left Palm Beach County for good. He said there have been many times that he wanted to return, but his surviving daughter forbade it.

Chris remained in contact with Ted Padich at the Sober Homes Task Force and also maintained strong views about federal laws that unwittingly contributed to his beloved daughter's demise. His main target was HIPAA, which Jenna's treatment providers invoked to keep him, her own father, in the dark. Chris fervently believed that parents of those with substance use disorders, which are diseases of the brain induced by chemical exposure, must be able to access the healthcare activities of enrolled adult family members.

"It all stems from the confidentiality laws," Chris said. "Parents have no control or even knowledge of their child's condition when they get trapped into the Florida Shuffle. The addiction treatment providers and marketers do not have to tell parents anything, and most often they will not."

Chris continued to seek justice for his daughter after her death. He implored law enforcement to find her killer and raised awareness of the Florida Shuffle by speaking with all who would listen. He wanted the world to know about Jenna's story so it could serve as a reminder that the lives lost from rehab industry corruption are more than mere statistics, and more than anonymous "junkies." They are someone's son or daughter. And their loss is soul-crushing to so many.

CHAPTER 10

HOPE

For Ted Padich and his Sober Homes Task Force investigators, a successful outcome can come in different forms. It can be quantified by the number of perpetrators arrested for their crimes, or the conviction rate at trial. It could be anecdotal evidence that unscrupulous sober home and drug treatment center owners have packed up and moved elsewhere—or decided never to set up shop in Palm Beach County in the first place. As much as the pain of failing to rescue the Jennas and Jamies from the abyss of the Florida Shuffle serves to motivate Padich and his team, a positive result—defined in many subjective ways—provides much-needed hope that their work is making a difference.

Why do some Florida Shuffle victims make it out alive, while others succumb to its vice-like grip? The fortunate ones often have a strong support system with relentless family members. But as Jamie Daniels' parents tragically learned, a close-knit, loving family provides no guarantee of success. Sometimes it is just the good fortune of reaching a loved one at the right time on the right day to convince them to leave the Florida freebies and return home. Whether it is persistence or pure luck, just calling the toll-free number of the Sober Homes Task Force can sometimes make the difference between life and death.

"Adam" and "Betty" lived in a medium-sized city in Ohio. Adam was born and raised there and had many of the same friends throughout his childhood and early teenage years. But his family, like many in the United States, was caught in the struggles of domestic turmoil, separation, and divorce. His biological father left home, divorcing his mother, when Adam was a young boy. Betty was not fond of being a single mother in a Midwest town. She found another partner and married him not long after that divorce. Adam lived with his mother and stepfather after their marriage, but he never warmed up to the new father figure in his life. Whether it was his hostility toward his stepfather, or just a relationship that failed for any of the myriad reasons that married people fail to honor their vows, Betty and Adam's stepfather separated and then divorced when he was in the tenth grade of high school. Betty was saddened by her second divorce, but Adam never shed a tear. It was more like "good riddance." During a series of interviews with Campbell, spread over the last three years, Betty asked that any information that could link her family's story back to her and her son be avoided, out of concern for privacy. [154]

The split-up caused Adam and Betty to move into the suburbs. She could not afford to stay in the house in the city where they had been living. That meant Adam had to attend a different high school with new friends, new surroundings, and new trouble to get into.

Betty described herself as completely naïve about her only child's foray into drugs. That was until her serenity bubble popped when Adam first overdosed. Betty remembered it all too well. It was on a Sunday that started like so many others in the dead of winter in their medium-sized Ohio city. The long, dreary, dark days of cold, wet, and miserable weather had sapped everyone's resilience, like it did every year at that time. The month of February had been particularly rainy and chilly, but no snow to speak of. So, when a light layer of wet snow blanketed the city the night before, it was an exceptional event for Adam and his friends. It was a reason to celebrate, as they did on so many other Saturday nights. Only two years out of his teens, Adam was a seasoned partier.

"Adam had started staying out late and breaking curfew," Betty told Campbell. He was giving his mother the cold shoulder again, just as he did during his drug-filled later teenage years. During the first of Campbell's several telephone interviews with Betty, when she told the story of Adam's overdose at her home, her comment about a curfew struck him as odd. As they spoke on the phone, he wondered how a twenty-year-old still had a curfew? Some other parts of the story did not add up, like why she allowed him to be a party animal and still live in her house and why he was not working and sharing the load with his mother. Campbell noticed that Betty was often vague and less than transparent when talking about her son's problems caused by a substance use disorder. She was also defensive.

By the time Adam was in his late teens and early twenties, Betty told Campbell that she was dismayed that she did not know any of his new friends, unlike the old days when he was still a child, when she knew their names, their parents' names, and shared in many of her son's after-school activities. "I knew he drank beer and partied with his friends," Betty said. "All through high school, and for a few years afterward, that was it. I never suspected that Adam or his friends were using drugs, not even marijuana. I thought that was the extent of it. Then one day . . . " She never finished the sentence and quickly changed the subject, as her voice dropped to a whisper. Betty's naïveté regarding her son's true lifestyle was a striking reflection of her parenting style. It seemed to Campbell that a deep, parental love for her son blocked out all potential negativity.

Perhaps a bit worried that she was being perceived as a pushover in her interview with Campbell, Betty told a story of Adam being pulled over, arrested, and taken to the county jail for driving under the influence (DUI) of alcohol. Betty admitted that Adam had been a binge drinker throughout his later teenage years, despite offering frequent motherly advice to her son about the hazards of excessive alcohol consumption.

After he graduated from high school, Betty hoped that her son had gone through the worst of his maladaptive behaviors. She said this to Campbell with a hint of regret in her voice: "He was just taking a long time growing up." Instead of coddling Adam after the DUI, Betty gave her son a dose of tough love.

That night, someone from the jailhouse called Betty, offering her the opportunity to pay the bail for his arrest and take him home. She recalled her heart nearly beating out of her chest when she took the phone call. Then, after calming down, she grew angry that her grown-up son had been so cavalier in driving after excessively drinking alcohol. She refused the offer, waiting until the next day to post bail and take Adam home. She gave him an earful on the way to the house, but he was not willing to hear any of it. The hungover Adam was arrogant, entitled, and discourteous to his mother. To this day, Campbell does not understand how she put up with his bad behavior.

To drill down on how or why Adam went from drinking with friends in high school to overdosing on drugs, Betty was asked how her parenting styles might have differed from that of Adam's father, who had joint custody, or even his stepfather who was in the picture until Adam was a sophomore in high school.

"Our parenting styles, mine and that of his [biological] father have some similarities," Betty said. "But our home environments and lifestyles are very different." She was strict on some issues, lenient on others, and vice versa. Between the two of them, it was easier for Adam to manipulate and lie to his mother—"and get away with it"—compared to his father. Adam's stepfather had no sway on Adam's upbringing other than being an irritant to the kid.

In her younger days, Betty had tried cigarettes and pot a few times but did not like them. She even tried cocaine in her mid-twenties, yet never touched any drugs after that. As she matured through her adult years, and developed the sense of responsibility that comes with being a parent, she grew to dislike everything about alcohol and illicit drug use. Her friends shared her traditional, conservative lifestyle choices and were never into drugs either.

Betty's abhorrence for alcohol and drug use was shaped in her childhood years. She lived through the trauma of being raised by, as she said, "an alcoholic father."

Betty's second husband never warmed up to Adam. They never formed any type of relationship and often butted heads. The animosity that Betty's second husband had toward her son was concealed in the early days of wedded bliss, but as the newness of the marriage faded, the anger and resentment spilled over and became obvious. By the time Adam was a teenager, the gloves were off, and irreconcilable differences existed between the stepson and stepfather.

"Adam moved in with his real dad during the summer between his sophomore and junior years of high school," Betty said, "which caused him to switch schools yet again." The partying continued through his senior year. Even the DUI, soon after graduating from high school, did not slow down Adam's dangerous lifestyle. Drugs, alcohol, go-carts, cars, girls, late nights—it was quite a social life for the midwesterner.

Adam did not go to college or learn a trade, despite his parents' pleas. He never had a real job, even after high school, but had his own apartment and was somehow paying his bills.

"A lot of times, though, he would borrow money from me, which in hindsight, was probably spent on drugs and stuff like that," Betty said. "That's what other people were saying to me. He came to live with us right after his grandma, my mom, died in 2017." It was not made clear why Adam chose to, or was told to, move out of his father's house, but his lifestyle and lack of a job may have had something to do with it. Adam brought a friend and moved into the house, assuring his mother that he was going to start his life over and get a job. But all Betty saw was partying. She told Campbell again that she had no idea her son was doing coke, Xanax, and other drugs.

The night of his overdose, Adam took an excessive number of Xanax pills and drank far too much alcohol. He was so out of it that Betty took him to the local hospital's emergency department. Thanks to quality medical care, he survived. Recognizing it was a close call, Adam agreed to enter a local drug detox program. A week later, Betty received a phone call from a social worker affiliated with Adam's treatment center. She told Betty that "Adam won the lottery. We're going to send him to Florida to a beautiful drug rehab facility, and we're paying for his plane ticket!"

Betty received photos of the facility that made it look like a country club. But her thoughts did not matter, as the fix was in. Adam was an adult and had already made the decision to accept the free, one-way trip to Florida. For Adam and Betty, the Florida Shuffle had arrived at their doorstep and was not leaving without a body.

With his one-way plane ticket in hand, Adam flew to the Florida treatment facility with high hopes from false promises. He liked the idea of beaches, palm trees, bikinis, and warm ocean waters—and especially because it cost him nothing. Just before he left, Adam confided to his mother that he had been supporting himself as a drug dealer, besides being a regular user. That sure explained how he got by without a job.

"It hit me like a ton of bricks," Betty said. "I experienced sharp pangs of guilt at being so ignorant of his actions." Overwhelmed by the situation, Betty felt abject helplessness as a passive observer rather than an active participant in Adam's life. He was an adult and used that fact like a cudgel over her head. He told his mother that he was in charge and was the one making his own life decisions.

Betty decided to make up for lost time and opportunity to engage in her son's life by learning about the world of detox, drug rehab, and sober homes. "I did a ton of research," she said, even as her family told her that he was a grown man who must make his own mistakes.

"I did not care what anybody said," Betty told us. "As a mother, I went with my gut. Every fiber in my body told me that the rehab process was fraudulent."

Betty observed that things were going awfully fast. She did not have any experience with rehab centers but was a medical coder/biller by profession. Betty asked herself, *why and how is he getting a free plane ride to Florida? How is that going to get billed through insurance? Who's paying for all this stuff?*

Betty started asking questions of his new rehab in Florida, but no one would give her information. According to Betty, the representatives would just say it was because of federal privacy laws, and because he was an adult with insurance through his father (Betty's ex-husband).

The lack of transparency raised more red flags. Fortunately, Betty and her ex-husband were on good speaking terms and he shared his online login credentials to view the medical bills being processed by his health insurance company for Adam's care. That was when she started seeing bills coming in for things that made no sense. She saw new prescription medications prescribed to her son who, prior to his overdose, was not on anything except the illicit drugs he was consuming. She developed a partial list of those medications and shared the information with Campbell, as part of their interview. There were at least ten to twelve prescriptions in all, including Haldol (used to fight schizophrenia), ADHD meds, naltrexone, antidepressants, anti-anxiety meds, and some for gastroesophageal reflux disease.

The next cause for suspicion was the incessant amount of phone calls made by administrators at the Florida drug rehab facility demanding that Betty pay up for Adam's care, even though the facility did not even allow her to speak with her son. She was not listed on his health insurance and was not financially responsible for him, but rehab personnel kept calling about billing issues anyway.

"I caught on within the first few weeks," she said. "All they really cared about was money. They did not give a hoot about helping Adam with his medical care."

Not sure what to do, Betty searched the internet for help and found the Palm Beach County Sober Homes Task Force toll-free number. She called the hotline and spoke to Chief Investigator Ted Padich about Adam's facility. In no uncertain terms, Padich told Betty to come down and get Adam out of there immediately. Otherwise, she would never see her son again because he would be dead, Padich bluntly told her.

Betty took Padich's warning seriously and rushed to pack an overnight bag. She left home at 4:00 p.m. and did not tell Adam's father that she was leaving for Florida. She just packed up and drove south, with her motherly instincts leading the way. Betty drove all night, downing cups of coffee, rolling down the windows for fresh air, and blasting the radio to stay awake.

She called the facility from the car but was stonewalled. Betty was told she could only speak with Adam during "family night," and only if she came in person. Of course, personnel at the rehab facility in Florida knew that Adam's mother lived out of state. They were being too clever by half.

"I didn't tell Adam I was coming, or anyone else," Betty said. "I was convinced I needed to surprise them, to get him out of there."

Betty had learned from her research that the last day of treatment is when rogue rehabs may encourage their patients to relapse. "On the final day, he would be offered money to buy drugs, so he could pee dirty," Betty said. "Then he would qualify for another stay in addiction treatment with his new friends. I had to save him before he entered the next phase."

At daybreak the next morning, she was still driving, and rolled the windows down to wake up. She noticed that it smelled different in Florida. Musky. Moist. Humid. She was on I-75, heading south. When she got on the Florida Turnpike, thoughts of saving her son perked her up. A few hours later, Betty could see cabbage palm trees and clumps of dull-green palmettos dotting the flat landscape, and knew she was getting close. As she passed the town of Port St. Lucie, Betty knew from her Maps phone app that she was only forty-five minutes north of Palm Beach County. She was excited, almost giddy. Soon thereafter, her cell phone lit up. It gave her a jolt, probably because she was hypercaffeinated and sleep deprived.

Betty thought, *It's the facility. Do I answer this? Do I tell them where I am?* She was nearing the drug rehab facility and knew the person on the other end of the line thought she was still home in Ohio. *What the heck.* She picked up the phone and answered. Just as she put the phone to her ear she looked to the west and saw a flock of white cattle egrets swirling around a herd of brown and white cows. *How cool. You don't see that back home,* she thought.

Maybe it was in response to Betty's tone, or her jitters from drinking coffee all night, but the representative on the line was rude. The representative wanted to know if she was able to attend the family night. Much to the rep's surprise, Betty said she was in town and would be at the facility in about an hour and a half.

"They're like, '*What?*'" Betty said in one of the interviews with Campbell. "I then asked them to put Adam on the phone." Betty's request was declined. Adam later told his mother that once the people in the facility learned she was so close, the entire staff panicked. They whisked him out of his room to tidy up and prepare for a visit.

As Betty pulled into the parking lot, she felt sick to her stomach. Maybe it was the fourth cup of coffee, or that she was parking in a rough-looking industrial strip mall rather than a nice medical facility, as promised. She thought, *What the heck did I just get myself involved in? This is dangerous.* Once parked, she quickly walked up to the front door.

Betty told the first employee she encountered that she was here to take Adam home, that he didn't need to be there any-more. Predictably, Betty got the run-around. She was told: "He's an adult. He needs to be here. You're going to ruin his progress."

"Blah, blah, blah," Betty derisively remarked while telling story. "I remained calm and stood my ground. I told the growing group of facility employees that if they didn't let him come with me, right now, I would call the police." She hadn't forgotten what Detective Padich had advised her to say—and to remain calm. She tried to appear calm but was terrified inside.

Attempting to control the quiver in her voice, Betty asked as politely as possible if she could just have a moment alone with her son. First, the staff would not allow it. After a tense stand-off at the front door, however, they finally gave in.

Betty was shocked but pleased when they acquiesced to a one-hour visit with Adam alone in her car, provided she prom-ised to bring him back. She knew that she was going to break that promise, and it was for good reason. It was only a few minutes before Adam shuffled out the front door with a cup of steaming hot coffee in his hand. Betty knew her son was glad to see her as they exchanged hugs, kisses, and tears before climbing into the car.

"We left the parking lot and drove around for a while," Betty said. "I told Adam the real purpose of my visit was to take him home because he was in danger." Adam was having nothing of it. He flatly refused to leave the facility and go back to Ohio with her. She was starting to lose her temper when Adam implored her to stay calm and drive him back to the facility. Back and forth they went, raising their voices, crying, and begging. Finally, Adam relented and said he would go home with her the next day.

Against her better judgment, Betty returned to the rehab facility. It was getting late in the evening and the mosquitoes were out in full force when they arrived back at the industrial park. It looked desolate, empty, and downright scary to Betty. To her surprise, one of the staff agreed that Adam could go home the following day, but not that night. It was only then that Betty learned Adam was not even sleeping at the facility, rather he was bused off-site to a sober home and driven to the rehab each morning. Adam claimed he did not know where the sober home was even located. He told his mother the first place he stayed in was an apartment complex with rampant drug use and cockroaches that scurried around the floor every night. After that place, he was shuttled among a variety of different sober homes, where the word "sober" meant nothing. Adam told his mother that everyone tried to sleep with one eye open so they would not be robbed blind, or worse.

The next morning, Adam rolled out of the bus, which they all called the "druggie buggy" with a garbage bag stuffed with dirty clothes and personal belongings. Betty had stayed overnight at a local motel. She arrived early to the drug rehab facility where she waited in the parking lot, sipping hot coffee and swatting mosquitoes. Her arms and neck looked like she had measles from all the bug bites. The discharge process took all day, even though Adam needed only his Ziploc bag of various medications and the garbage bag full of his belongings.

A staff member begrudgingly discharged Adam and made plans for him to stay at what was called a "halfway house" back in Ohio. Betty had to promise she would have him at the house within twenty-four hours, which meant another all-nighter on the road. When they finally got into the car for the long drive home, Adam pulled out the big Ziploc bag containing several prescription meds in various brightly colored plastic bottles. She was not sure what he took, but Adam slept the entire twenty-hour drive home.

For the next six months, Adam lived in that halfway house while trying to hold down a few odd jobs. His girlfriend had dumped him when he left for Florida, but they rekindled their relationship when he returned to town, and it did not take long for her to become pregnant. After they received the news, the couple decided to get engaged. He told his mother that it was "for the baby's sake." Adam moved out of the halfway house to live with his fiancé, but they split up after the baby arrived. To his mother's knowledge, Adam remained sober before the breakup, but she had been wrong before. He had been working at a good job to support his family, but after the relationship ended, Adam again moved away from his hometown. His mother was told it was to escape years of bad memories.

Adam survived the Florida Shuffle, but the talons of drug addiction do not easily release to allow for fairy tale endings. According to his mother, Adam now lives under his father's roof and works hard but has returned to smoking pot and is probably using other drugs again.

"It's hard to get in touch with him most days," Betty said, "but life goes on."

Betty was one of many anxious mothers of young adults with substance use disorder to find hope in the Sober Homes Task Force. Ted Padich and his team are comforted by the small victories, such as Betty reuniting with her son, despite Adam's apparent relapse. What really buoys their spirits are the success stories they can see with their own eyes. Such as the time that one of the Task Force detectives received a desperate call from Erin in Pennsylvania about her son, "John."

Some of Erin's friends described her parenting style as that of a helicopter mom, hovering over her son with radar scanning for danger. Erin felt she needed to be that way, especially after her son developed an opioid use disorder. As part of a probation requirement on an earlier drug-related conviction, John was required to seek addiction treatment and, like so many others, he was marketed down to Florida. Not exactly a rule follower, John was soon kicked out of the facility, which triggered a probation violation and an arrest warrant back in Pennsylvania.

In search of her son, Erin reached out to multiple rehabs and sober homes only to be repeatedly rebuffed. Unscrupulous operators and landlords financially depend on willing victims like John and know that a parent in far-away Pennsylvania is in no position to do anything about it, so they ignored her. Refusing to allow the Florida Shuffle to win, Erin scoured the internet for help, which is how she found out about the Sober Homes Task Force and its hotline.

Erin called the toll-free number and reached Detective Robert McGinley. With a voice of desperation and determination, Erin told the detective that she thought John was being brokered to treatment centers and sober homes, and she worried that his next drug hit would be his last. Erin knew that her son was with a girlfriend he met in rehab who used opioids with him as they traveled from place to place. Detective McGinley asked Erin if John had been leaving any clues about his current location. Did she have any credit card charges, cell phone bills, or social media posts? After some thought, Erin told him that she had discovered an Uber receipt and learned that it was from a trip that John took to a sober home in Lantana. She asked if the detective could follow up on this lead. For McGinley, it was worth a shot. Address in hand, the detective drove to the house and knocked on the door. A young woman answered the door who matched the description of John's girlfriend.

He introduced himself as Detective McGinley from the Sober Homes Task Force, and asked if her boyfriend, John, was around. Overhearing the conversation, a shirtless man with unkempt hair suddenly appeared at the door, matching John's description.

"John, your mother called me because she loves you, she worries about you, and she desperately needs you to come home," Detective McGinley said. "Please don't make me have to tell her that her son is dead from an overdose."

John did not respond right away. He silently took it all in. He seemed stunned that this physically imposing detective with a badge and firearm was not trying to arrest, handcuff, or scream at him. Instead, McGinley was appealing to John as a father would to a wayward son. The detective knew John was his mother's entire world and could tell that her son shared the same affection in return.

McGinley offered to put John on a plane to fly home to face the probation violation charges back in Pennsylvania. McGinley assured the intimidated young man that if he got back into rehab there, he would tell the local district attorney in Pennsylvania about John's cooperation. McGinley reasoned with John that a call from the Sober Homes Task Force would likely convince the prosecutor to give him rehabilitation instead of incarceration.

In response, John asked if he could talk to his girlfriend in private. During the chat, she refused to leave the co-ed drug den, forcing John to make a life-altering decision. Fortunately, he chose wisely. He packed up his belongings and left with McGinley for Palm Beach International Airport.

An overjoyed Erin soon reunited with her son in Pennsylvania, who faced the music back at home when he turned himself in to the authorities. True to his word, Detective McGinley spoke to the local district attorney, who compassionately allowed John to enter treatment in place of jail time.

Later, Detective McGinley went back to investigate the co-ed sober home that was so appealing to John's now ex-girlfriend only to find it had closed. That brief visit from the Sober Homes Task Force was enough to convince the operator to pack up and leave town. There was no word of what happened to the residents, including the ex-girlfriend.

Two years later, Detective McGinley received a heartfelt thank you letter from Erin. In it, she gave an inspiring update on her son's recovery. It read:

Officer McGinley,

Two years ago, you and your partner helped me find my son and get him back to PA. (He was in Florida for rehab and relapsed.) Something tells me you remember him because we are just miles away from your hometown.

I wanted to let you know today is two years since you helped me get him on a plane. And although he got high before leaving, it was his last time getting high—he has been clean ever since that flight home. Granted, he has legal issues but has faced them, pays his fines, is on probation. He has a job working for the Laborer's Union. He will be applying for an apprenticeship in the heavy equipment operator's union as soon as he gets his driver's license back.

NONE of these would have been possible without your help. I tell everyone how I have two angels in Florida [McGinley and Ted Padich] and how they saved my son. Well, everyone but John. I have yet to tell him how the events rolled out but will one day. You saved my son and for this you will always have a special spot in my heart. Perhaps if you ever come to visit family in PA, we can take you to dinner.

Thank you, my dear angels!!!

Erin

CHAPTER 11

THE GOOSE THAT LAID THE GOLDEN EGGS

Although well-intentioned, federal law has enabled and exacerbated the Florida Shuffle. The early foundations for fraud and abuse in the drug rehab and sober home industry had already been constructed by the time President Obama signed the ACA into law in 2010. Two years before, the Mental Health Parity and Addiction Equity Act expanded benefits for drug treatment in most health insurance policies. The Fair Housing Amendments Act of 1988 supplemented the prior Fair Housing Act by making it illegal to discriminate against individuals with physical or mental disabilities. The Americans with Disabilities Act of 1990 classified as disabled many individuals who are addicted to drugs or in recovery, thereby protecting them from discrimination. Taken together, the ADA and the Fair Housing Amendments Act protect sober homes from regulatory harassment, which many interpret as preventing mandatory inspections, certification, or registration.

Desperate families with loved ones in drug rehab have been thwarted in their attempts to communicate because of the Health

Insurance Portability and Accountability Act (HIPAA). Enacted in 1996, HIPAA is intended to protect sensitive patient health information from falling into the wrong hands, but it has been used as an excuse for shady rehabs to keep families in the dark.

An unusual convergence of disparate political ideologies also played a role in creating the Florida Shuffle. For years, many conservatives had concerns that institutionalizing people with mental or behavioral health issues was too expensive. Many liberals felt that institutionalizing those with mental illness was inhumane. Common ground from these divergent frames of reference led to the reduction of mental health hospitals and public treatment beds. The result was a booming industry of private addiction treatment rehabs to fill the void.

In 2013, the year before the ACA's major coverage provisions went into effect, significant swaths of America were caught up in the opioid dragon's grip, and many were part of the forty-four million Americans who lacked health insurance. Help was on the way, however, and in just three years, the number of uninsured Americans dropped to an historic low. But just as the well-intended and long-overdue crackdown on pill mills and opioid diversion led to the rise in illicit heroin use and, soon thereafter, fentanyl and its analogs, it was the ACA's noble goal of expanded insurance coverage and increased access to addiction treatment that, ironically, led to the Florida Shuffle.

The ACA has done a lot of good by expanding the availability of drug treatment to millions of Americans who battle addiction, but it is being exploited by corrupt providers who encourage an endless cycle of relapse because they get reimbursed on a fee-for-service basis: the more the treatments fail, the more they keep getting paid.

For years, health insurance companies largely ignored this crisis, choosing to pay dubious claim after dubious claim rather than pushing back as the first line of defense against fraud. Despite their sizable anti-fraud divisions, with investigators and number-crunchers specially trained to identify and deny suspicious claims, insurer largesse has been the Florida Shuffle's lifeblood. And the main reason why so many insurers have been lackadaisical about fighting overbilling and overutilization in the drug treatment industry stems from the same federal law that unwittingly created the Florida Shuffle to begin with: the ACA.

In reality, the law that is truly responsible for the Florida Shuffle is actually the Law of Unintended Consequences. Just as the nationwide crackdown on prescription opioids led to the heroin and fentanyl crises, and federal laws designed to help individuals overcome substance use disorder inadvertently incentivized their exploitation, insurance reforms meant to prioritize treatment over corporate profits have reduced the motivation to combat fraud.

The official website of the Affordable Care Act, HealthCare.gov, says that the ACA's "80/20 Rule" (also known as the medical loss ratio, or MLR) is designed to "hold insurance companies accountable and help keep your costs down." As the website explains:

> *The 80/20 Rule generally requires insurance companies to spend at least eighty percent of the money they take in from premiums on healthcare costs and quality improvement activities. The other twenty percent can go to administrative, overhead, and marketing costs.*

> *If an insurance company uses 80 cents out of every premium dollar to pay for your medical claims and activities that improve the quality of care, the company has a Medical Loss Ratio of eighty percent . . .*
>
> *If your insurance company doesn't meet these requirements, you'll get a rebate on part of the premium that you paid.*[155]

When the government refers to the insurance company's 20 percent for "administrative, overhead, and marketing costs," it also means corporate profits. (The conspicuous absence of the controversial word, "profits," is an example of careful political marketing.) Since the ACA limits an insurance company's share of each premium dollar to 20 percent, an increase in premiums is a sure way to increase profits. When the payout side of the pie (the other 80 percent) expands, the insurer's share increases as well. That is, the more a company pays out in claims, the more profits it can keep.

This can lead to some perverse incentives such as a possible financial windfall for insurers who pay inflated claims to corrupt providers. At the very least, the 80/20 rule suppressed an insurance company's fraud-fighting libido. Rather than harming the bottom line, an excessive reimbursement for an unnecessary urinalysis could be paid by raising premiums to all other policyholders, with the company allowed to keep 20 percent of the extra payments.

One commentator described the unintended consequences of the 80/20 rule as "[t]he higher the cost, the greater the take," allowing insurance companies to "benefit off the increase of disease. They will jack up rates and continue to benefit from the overproduction of high cost and even unnecessary medical procedures. The more that medical services cost, the greater the dollars in their cut, long term."[156]

Ted Padich believes the 80/20 rule, along with a fear of lawsuits for slow or insufficient payments, made insurance companies reluctant to examine and deny suspicious claims, preferring instead to pay first and then "claw back" some excessive reimbursements later.

Another explanation for insurer inaction is that the companies were unprepared for the sudden surge of claims arising from the implementation of the ACA provisions to expand access to addiction treatment. Insurers had long refused or limited coverage for behavioral health conditions, including substance use disorders, so when the ACA suddenly made drug rehab a growth industry, the anti-fraud divisions were caught flat-footed. In Detective Padich's twenty-two years of experience fighting insurance fraud, he learned that "insurance companies don't really read the bills that providers send to them. They usually just pay it. A human being may never see the bill. They have algorithms designed to thwart this kind of fraud, but they don't always work when it comes to drug rehab billing. So, the same company that would call you three times if you tripped down the stairs at the office to make sure it wasn't a workers' comp claim doesn't do the same when it comes to people in drug treatment. They would rather pay the bill and later try to claw the money back after an investigation than get sued for not paying for drug treatment."[157]

Denise Corbisiero, chief operating officer of Integrity Billing, which represents drug treatment centers in billing disputes with insurance companies, agreed that insurers knew little about covering substance use disorder until the ACA suddenly required them to do so. Since there is no universal scientific protocol for treating addiction, befuddled insurers were flooded with bills from thousands of different providers within a newfangled subcategory of behavioral health.

Even after the insurers finally came up to speed on the reality of fraudulent billings, Corbisiero said basic market forces continue to make the companies err on the side of paying dubious claims: "Employers and unions pay a lot of money to get coverage for their people, and if insurers start pulling in the reins and refusing care, these large groups are going to look for policies somewhere else." The insurers fear losing their share of the lucrative group health insurance market if too many policyholders complain about nonpayment or underpayment of claims, which is why the companies prefer to approve questionable charges first before clawing some of it back later. Plus, with the 80/20 rule and the ability to raise premiums across policyholders, insurance industry profits remain strong and stable.[158]

When Dave Aronberg testified before the U.S. House Subcommittee on Oversight and Investigations Committee in December 2017, congressional members specifically asked about the insurance industry's role in combating fraud. Although they were taken aback to learn that the 80/20 rule had helped feed the Florida Shuffle—with audible sounds of dismay filling the committee room—as of this writing there has been no attempt to fix the problem or to align the ACA's financial incentives with quality care.

One insurer that aggressively tried to thwart the Florida Shuffle was Centene Health Net of Arizona, now known as Arizona Complete Health Care, which investigated the state's drug treatment industry after its payments ballooned from $2.4 million in 2014 to $47.4 million in 2015—more than any other type of medical care in the state. Much of the boom occurred in the city of Prescott, which had a population of just over 40,000, but claimed more than one hundred sober homes. The investigation spooked several Prescott sober-home owners enough that they closed their doors for good. In 2016, six treatment centers in Prescott and three in Scottsdale sued Centene Health Net after the company slowed and stopped reimbursements it flagged as suspicious. In response, the insurer countersued the plaintiffs, alleging widespread fraud.[159] The litigation ended in a settlement two years later.[160]

Centene Health Net's counterclaim accused "teams of brokers" of recruiting out-of-state patients to fraudulently obtain insurance policies and seek treatment in Arizona. The insurer cited examples of people lured from California, Indiana, New Jersey, New York, Tennessee, and Wisconsin, who falsely represented that they lived in Prescott or Scottsdale. Body brokers allegedly scouted these prospects from homeless shelters, jails, and Alcoholics Anonymous meetings and referred them to the highest-bidding treatment center. If the patient did not have insurance, or if the facility was not part of the insurer's network, the rehab would surreptitiously pay the insurance premiums, deductibles, and co-payments.[161]

This type of marketing scheme was so widespread in New England that Massachusetts Attorney General (now Governor)

Maura Healey issued a public warning to residents against traveling to "so-called 'treatment centers' in Arizona, California, or Florida." Healy cited multiple reports of rehabs in the three states providing "little or no care to patients," along with marketers that "have stopped paying insurance premiums, which has resulted in patients getting removed from treatment facilities and stranded" thousands of miles from home.[162]

For years, urinalysis billing drove the fraud until it became so excessive, obvious, and egregious that the corrupt players finally killed the goose that laid the golden eggs. Forced awake from their slumber by widespread fraud that caught the attention of law enforcement, state regulators, and grieving families, insurance companies dramatically reduced reimbursements for urine testing. In response, corrupt providers and labs billed excessive amounts for "confirmatory drug testing," which is a secondary test that provides a positive identification of a specific substance.[163] After insurers caught on to that abuse, many bad actors moved to lucrative allergy and genetic testing to stay one step ahead. The cat and mouse game continues to this day.

CHAPTER 12

SOLUTIONS

Although Palm Beach County's crackdown on corruption in the drug treatment and sober home industry has been successful, it too has had an unintended consequence: Many rogue providers have fled the area to other communities that remain unprepared for what awaits them.

As the Sober Homes Task Force arrested rogue providers and shuttered corrupt facilities, Ted Padich and his team witnessed a game of Whac-A-Mole, where the criminal element left Palm Beach County for other communities unaware of the problem. To help combat the Florida Shuffle as it metastasizes, the Task Force has held training sessions for prosecutors and law enforcement officials throughout the state and has provided assistance to jurisdictions in other parts of the country.

Palm Beach County's approach to fighting the Florida Shuffle can be replicated in every community in every state. Dave Aronberg and Alan Johnson have traveled the country to speak to the respective trade organizations for drug treatment providers and insurance companies to raise awareness of the Florida

Shuffle and have provided guidance to the National Association of Insurance Commissioners, which is comprised of regulators from all fifty states. Still, the issue has largely been ignored at the national level. Until the federal government takes significant action, local authorities will be forced to continue fighting this crisis with one hand tied behind their backs. Only Washington, DC, has the power to turn off the spigot of fraud and abuse that continues to flow down into our neighborhoods in the form of corrupt drug rehabs and flophouses masquerading as sober homes.

The first step to solving this problem at the national level is to tweak the ACA to adopt an outcome-based reimbursement model. It is critical to incentivize recovery rather than relapse by rewarding the legitimate, effective treatment providers while penalizing the others. Currently, the opposite is true. The big money is more likely to flow to the substandard providers, not the best ones.

Ironically, the possible solution to the Florida Shuffle lies within the very same federal law that helped create the crisis. The ACA changed Medicare to reduce payments to hospitals with high readmission rates while providing bonuses to providers that achieve high scores on patient outcome and care experiences. Yet, this policy of linking quality to payment does not apply to private insurers who pay for drug rehab services.

When policymakers decide the future of the ACA, they should extend Medicare's outcome-based reimbursement model to the world of private insurance payments for drug rehabilitation. This could reward the best recovery centers while shuttering rogue operators who give false promises and illicit benefits to patients, then siphon precious resources into treating and then encouraging repeated relapses.

Reforming the current fee-for-service model should also improve patient outcomes by incentivizing a longer-term, lower-level care model instead of the current short-term, intensive programs that may have as low as a 10 percent success rate. Studies show that a decelerated recovery period over twelve months is both cheaper and more successful than the current model.[164] Scientists found that longer-term care resulted in increased treatment engagement, higher rates of abstinence, and less homelessness after discharge.[165] We have come to accept repeated relapses as an automatic detour toward recovery, but it doesn't have to be that way.

Another needed fix to end the Florida Shuffle involves clarifying the Americans with Disabilities Act. The ADA requires state and local governments, including homeowner associations (HOAs), to provide "reasonable accommodations" to individuals with disabilities, including those recovering from addiction who are not using drugs. Weighing on the minds of local government officials are the experiences of Newport Beach, California,[166] and Boca Raton, Florida, both of which had to pay millions of dollars to owners of sober homes after city ordinances improperly regulated them, violating the ADA.[167]

Since the ADA exempts sober homes from most local government and HOA regulations, three or more residents can legally be squeezed into every bedroom of a single-family home. If a city ordinance or HOA rule limits the number of unrelated people from residing in a single-family home—as is often the case—the sober-home operator just points to the federal ADA and requests a "reasonable accommodation" under the law to accommodate his residents in recovery. Almost always, city and HOA officials will quickly relent before they are hit with an expensive ADA lawsuit in federal court.

Local and state governments may not ban or refuse reasonable accommodation requests from sober homes seeking an exemption from many local codes and ordinances. This protection against discrimination, however, has a sinister side by allowing unethical sober-home owners to jeopardize the health and safety of their residents while using the ADA to shield their wrongdoing.

Anyone can operate a sober home. The best of sober homes are the ones you never even notice to be amongst you. The worst homes degenerate into flophouses, where unscrupulous landlords exploit people with substance use disorder for money or sex and allow or even encourage drug use. The well-appointed recovery residence, owned and operated by a humanitarian to help those recovering from addiction transition back into society, has ADA protection. So does a con artist's co-ed dorm with nine people "in recovery" stuffed into just three bedrooms with no standards or supervision and receiving kickbacks from corrupt treatment providers.

That is why Congress should urge the United States Department of Justice (DOJ) and the U.S. Department of Housing and Urban Development (HUD) to clarify the ADA to allow local governments to uphold national standards and best practices in sober homes for protecting residents in recovery.[168] The ADA does not need to be amended, just explained. In fact, the DOJ and HUD already attempted such a clarification back in November 2016, but their joint statement involved mostly zoning issues and only added to the confusion.[169]

Congress can fix the Florida Shuffle by tweaking the ACA and clarifying the ADA but has either not understood or cared about the problem—or both. On two separate occasions, Aronberg testified before congressional committees to highlight the loopholes, gaps, and abuses in federal law that continue to increase the death toll from the opioid crisis and has urged immediate action—to no avail.

With federal regulation lacking and Congress largely asleep at the wheel, two national entities have tried to fill the void: Oxford House and the National Alliance of Recovery Residences. Oxford Houses are residences chartered by a national nonprofit organization that applies strict rules and conditions attendant upon membership. These rules include sobriety, collective self-governance, the need to look out for each other, and "good neighbor" policies. Every resident has a voice—which means allowing for frequent voting on all important household decisions. Its founder and longtime CEO, Paul Molloy, who died in 2022, was in recovery himself, and found his sobriety through the Oxford House model.[170] They currently report over 3,200 self-sustaining sober houses utilizing their model, with more than 46,000 individuals living in an Oxford House during the year.[171]

Another leader in the field, the National Alliance of Recovery Residences (NARR), has developed model rules and standards for sober homes that various state nonprofit certifying entities adopt. Its affiliate, the Florida Association of Recovery Residences (FARR), has authorization by statute to certify recovery residences in the Sunshine State. Certification requires quality standards, including core principles of a recovery-based/ drug-free environment, management by a certified recovery residence administrator, a good neighbor policy, ethics and safety standards, resident rights and obligations, and a displacement policy when a resident materially violates these standards.

Since mandatory sober home certification was seen as a no-go under the ADA and FHAA, the Florida legislature made FARR certification voluntary, which means that most sober homes in Florida remain uncertified. State law, however, incentivizes certification by outlawing referrals to and from sober homes that are not FARR-certified.

Safe and sober housing is the key to long-term sobriety, yet the lack of nationwide standards in housing has actively contributed to the recycling of patients in and out of treatment. That is why federal law must change to allow state and local governments to require certification under NARR or similar standards (such as in Oxford Houses) to protect the vulnerable residents living in sober homes.

The federal government also needs to get tough on interstate marketing fraud. Misleading advertising is the proverbial tip of the Florida Shuffle's spear. Providers spend millions of dollars on online marketing to create a funnel from areas across the country to treatment destinations such as Florida, Arizona, Texas, and California. In many cases, investigators have found phone numbers and maps of legitimate addiction treatment providers hijacked by unscrupulous marketers. Online positioning in one geographic area can mislead the caller into thinking a facility is local when the local phone number is, in reality, a Trojan Horse, answered by a lead generator and sold downstream to the highest bidder. These phone calls are extremely valuable. A downstream lead-generated call may cost a facility $1,000 or more once insurance is validated.

Dave Aronberg thought that no amount of chicanery could surprise him after all the fraud and abuse he witnessed in the drug treatment industry. Then he received a tip that the phone number in the Google search results for the Florida Alcohol and Drug Abuse Association (FADAA)—a respected nonprofit association representing treatment providers—had been hijacked by a marketer who was steering unaware callers to rehabs that likely offered lucrative kickbacks. The fact that even a reputable trade association that tried to help the public identify legitimate providers was itself being exploited by shady players showed that no one is completely safe from the far-reaching tentacles of the Florida Shuffle's poison.

In 2017, Florida enacted landmark legislation to get tough on the false, misleading, and abusive practices in the marketing of addiction services, making them criminal and civil violations of state law.[172] Many fraudulent marketers, however, are operating on a regional or national level, and jurisdictional and investigatory limitations severely hinder effective state action. The lack of resources is also a problem. Local law enforcement is not equipped to investigate large marketing firms operating over state lines. Federal agencies, from the DOJ to the Federal Trade Commission (FTC), need to start holding abusive interstate marketers and marketing systems to task, both civilly and criminally.

As a practical matter, only substantial misdeeds that exceed monetary thresholds typically get the attention of federal prosecutors and regulators. The fly-by-night companies and lower-level frauds are largely off their radar. Aronberg's office investigated kingpin Kenny Chatman until federal prosecutors from the Southern District of Florida asked to take over the investigation of his multi-million-dollar scheme that involved human trafficking, money laundering, and healthcare fraud. Upon Chatman's arrest, the acting U.S. Attorney for the Southern District of Florida, Benjamin Greenberg, called Chatman's actions "egregious," excoriating Chatman for giving drugs to addicts and using "his position of power to sexually exploit his patients."[173] Likewise, the feds charged Dr. Michael Ligotti, the ubiquitous medical director for more than fifty different addiction treatment facilities, after his alleged healthcare fraud scheme reached $681 million over a decade.[174]

But even if the federal government adopts all these recommendations, and even if communities around the country start their own sober home task forces, the Florida Shuffle will continue if state laws ignore the real and present danger of patient brokering. An overwhelming number of criminal prosecutions take place at the local, rather than the national level, and several states lack the necessary laws to hold corrupt marketers, providers, and treatment center operators accountable.

In 2018, for example, local and state leaders in California reached out to Aronberg and Johnson for help. Rogue sober homes were littering the landscape and leading to a surge in overdose deaths. In particular, there was one scandal that reverberated across the country and rocked the Golden State's recovery industry to its core.

Evan Wright reported on the saga in *The Daily Beast* in 2019.

In 2012, self-described psychotherapist Christopher Bathum started Community Recovery in Los Angeles with a single treatment center. By 2016, it had mushroomed into two dozen facilities in California and Colorado with a total of four hundred beds. Insurance reimbursements mandated by federal law fueled the growth of Bathum's business. If patients did not have health insurance, the facility bought policies for them without their knowledge. For indigent patients in desperate need of treatment, this was not a source of concern, but rather an acceptable accommodation that kept the doors open for all.[175]

In late 2015, a newspaper reporter outed Bathum as a fraud and a felon. He was not a psychotherapist. In fact, he never finished college. Prior to founding his rehab business, Bathum had been a pool cleaner who had four felonies on his rap sheet for committing online fraud. Many individuals in the rehab industry have overcome drug addiction themselves, but Bathum's penchant for meth and heroin continued while he operated his treatment facilities. Just a few weeks before publication of the damaging article, Bathum overdosed in a Malibu motel while shooting up drugs with patients, but survived.[176]

Bathum's coziness with his vulnerable clients allegedly crossed the line in other ways. One former patient filed a lawsuit claiming that Bathum offered her drugs in exchange for sex, while others came forward to claim that Bathum had sexually assaulted them.[177]

Despite these well-publicized scandals, Bathum's rehab centers remained open for business. California officials maintained that they had no authority to regulate, inspect, or even enter Bathum's facilities because he ran them as unlicensed sober homes, and thus were protected by the ADA. Although the sober homes were not allowed to provide therapy or medical treatment, state authorities did not know what was going on inside because of ADA rules.[178]

As a result, it was business as usual for Bathum and his facilities after the newspaper exposé, even though a former employee previously presented state authorities with evidence of Bathum's drug use, sexual exploitation, past felonies, and fake credentials. The former employee also reported that Bathum gave patients heroin and meth, and sexually assaulted at least three individuals in his care. Finally, nearly a year after the news story, two years after the whistleblower came forward, and after at least seventeen patients died of overdoses at his facilities, Bathum was arrested in November 2016 and his business shut down.[179]

In February 2018, Bathum was found guilty of thirty-one counts of rape, sexual exploitation, and drug dealing.[180] He was sentenced to more than fifty-two years in prison, as well as a concurrent twenty years in prison for falsely billing health insurers $175 million, which included charging former clients after their treatment ended and obtaining insurance policies for patients without their knowledge.[181]

Thus, as Florida was cleaning up the corruption in the drug treatment industry, the Los Angeles area was earning the nickname of the "The Rehab Riviera." At the invitation of State Senator Pat Bates, Alan Johnson traveled to Sacramento to urge California legislators to pass much-needed legislation against patient brokering, which, shockingly, was not a state crime.

Despite what seemed like a favorable reaction to his testimony, Johnson watched in disbelief when the California legislature passed the bill only after its criminal penalties were stripped away. Thus, in California, rehab centers can no longer pay third parties to send them patients, but the punishment is limited to a fine or a possible license revocation.[182]

Even worse, the California law does not apply to sober homes, which are not even required to abide by the watered-down patient brokering rules for drug treatment centers. An attempt in 2020 by Sen. Bates to extend the patient brokering statute to sober homes was rejected after opposition from members of the nonprofit group, Disability Rights California. The group took the position that the 2020 bill "'crosses over the line' and violates state and federal fair housing laws that prohibit discrimination against the disabled."[183]

Local officials in California's Orange County thought they had finally made some progress in 2023 when Assembly member Kate Sanchez's bill, called the Sober Living Accountability Act, passed unanimously out of both legislative chambers. The legislation imposed new rules on sober homes that contract with county governments to, among other things, adopt the NARR code of ethics, establish written policies to allow residents to access MAT, and provide proof that the reversal agent, Narcan, is available and that staff is trained to administer it.[184]

The legislation was a baby step for California, but still represented progress in creating basic quality standards in the unregulated sober home industry. The unanimous vote was likely attributable, at least in part, to the Act's modest reach, as it would have only applied to sober homes that provided government services.[185]

The Act's limited application, simple goals, and unanimous legislative support still did not sway Governor Gavin Newsom, who vetoed the measure. In his veto message, the Governor noted that privately-owned recovery residences are not supervised or regulated by the state, and thus imposing new requirements on them would "create confusion among people seeking recovery services" to believe that sober homes are now licensed and certified facilities. In other words, California should not establish guidelines for sober homes because residents could mistakenly believe that the state is providing oversight and quality control, which it is not.[186]

In contrast to California's legislative lethargy and rampant infighting, one of the reasons for the success of Palm Beach County's Sober Homes Task Force was in bringing together all the stakeholders, government officials, and interested parties to break through the mistrust and accomplish the common goal of protecting vulnerable individuals in drug rehab. Disability rights activists need assurances that government oversight over the drug treatment and sober home industry is not meant to discriminate, but to save lives and promote a lasting sobriety. Unfortunately, town hall meetings can degenerate into NIMBY ("Not in My Backyard") wars, which fuel the doubts over government motivations and lead to federal lawsuits.

When the civilian side of the Sober Homes Task Force began meeting, a representative from the Palm Beach County League of Cities—which strongly opposed the unabated proliferation of sober homes—decried the participation of several sober home operators, whom he viewed as the enemy. The Task Force, however, embraced the big-tent approach and gained valuable intelligence about sober homes from insiders who wanted to clean up the industry because the miscreants had given everyone a bad name. Months later, when the Task Force unanimously issued its first set of recommendations, the same League of Cities representative forgot he had ever uttered a bad word about his fellow participants. Fighting the Florida Shuffle requires an all-hands-on-deck approach, and community outreach, communication, and transparency go a long way.

CHAPTER 13

HOW TO FIND THE RIGHT TREATMENT CENTER

The number one question we get asked by families confronting the realities of addiction is: "How do we find the right rehab for my loved one?" Because the drug treatment industry is so decentralized and lightly regulated, families are often uncertain on where to turn and whom to trust. Our hope is that the information provided in this chapter can help direct families to the right treatment center and recovery housing. Researching answers to these questions, rather than relying on a simple Google search—or even worse—a free plane ticket or other illegal incentive from a marketer, will keep families on the right track.

Recommendations for Drug Treatment Programs

Since 1978, the National Association of Treatment Providers (NAATP) has been a leading nonprofit professional society of top treatment providers. In 2018, Dave Aronberg was a guest speaker at the NAATP's National Leadership Addiction Conference and was impressed at the commitment to ethics within the association. Led by well-respected CEO Marvin Ventrell, whose career has focused on advocating for individuals battling addiction, the

NAATP has willingly lost hundreds of thousands of dollars in membership fees by booting treatment centers from its association that failed to meet its high ethical standards.

The organization disseminates best practices to the recovery industry and recommends that potential patients and their families approach drug treatment as they would other medical conditions. Ideally, this means asking for a recommendation from a family doctor or other medical professional. As an alternative, the association recommends speaking with your insurance company for in-network providers.

The NAATP also recommends that potential patients and their families perform the following due diligence before choosing a drug treatment provider. They should look for:

- Providers that are members of the NAATP[187] and accredited by the Commission on Accreditation of Rehabilitation Facilities (CARF)[188] or by the Joint Commission[189] and are state-licensed for all levels of care they provide. The state licensing authority and accrediting body will have records of complaints filed against a facility, and violations. Many of these resources are available online.

- Providers that seek in-depth patient medical history to assess appropriateness of fit. This information is critical in identifying appropriate levels of care, or patient needs that would be better addressed at alternate facilities. Be wary of providers only interested in your financial information.

- A center that is "in network" with your insurance. If not, ask what expenses you will incur.

- Programs that use evidence-based addiction treatment

practices ranging from MAT to twelve-step facilitation.

- Providers that have detailed information about staff qualifications and service types. While ancillary services, spa amenities, and destination locations are attractive, evidence-based clinical services and professionally credentialed staff are far more important for successful outcomes.

- Facilities that have bios for their staff, including medical and clinical personnel. They should show their location and provide detailed information about their assessment, treatment planning, and clinical services. Be wary of providers that offer generic answers you want to hear.

- Providers who offer detailed information about patient financial responsibility and billing practices. Although "free" sounds good, medical services have associated patient responsibilities through deductibles and copays. Be wary of facilities offering no out-of-pocket cost with insurance. If a provider offers free travel, help obtaining insurance, or any other substantive gift or incentive, this is a sign of potential insurance fraud and illegal patient brokering.[190]

NAATP'S QUESTIONS TO ASK POTENTIAL TREATMENT CENTERS

Finding safe, effective addiction treatment is not as easy as shopping online for household goods or figuring out where to go for vacation. Ted Padich's blood pressure rises every time he hears about someone who chose a facility based on a cursory internet search. It is imperative for families to conduct due diligence, which means asking the potential treatment centers many or all of the following questions:

- Are you state licensed, and for what levels of care?
- Are you accredited? If so, by whom? What services have been accredited?
- Are you a member of the NAATP?
- How long has the facility been in operation?
- Do you have a medical director on staff? Are they certified by the American Society of Addiction Medicine (ASAM)?
- What are the staff's qualifications?
- Are staff on-site and awake 24/7?
- Are licensed staff available 24/7?
- What qualifications do your clinicians have? Are group and individual counseling sessions provided by master's-level staff? Do clinicians have specialized training in treating substance use disorder?
- What are the facility's placement criteria?
- Can the facility treat the specific needs of the patient? Are they licensed and qualified to do so? Under what conditions will a patient be discharged or referred to alternate care?
- What is your procedure for referring to other treatment providers?
- Does the facility treat other medical and mental health conditions? Is it credentialed to do so?

- What evidence-based practices are used?

- How often are drug screens conducted? Does the facility follow ASAM guidelines for drug testing?

- Does the facility provide family counseling? How, and are there additional costs associated?

- What types of support services are provided after treatment? Does the provider have an alumni program? What types of discharge planning are used?

- Is the facility in-network with your insurance? What out of pocket costs will be assessed? How are these costs calculated?[191]

RECOMMENDATIONS FOR SOBER HOMES/RECOVERY RESIDENCES

Whether they are called sober homes, sober-living homes, recovery residences, or something else, the U.S. Government's SAMHSA set forth the following ten guiding principles, including best practices and minimum standards, for living environments that support individuals in recovery from addiction.[192] As a reminder, these residences are substance-free group homes that are distinct from inpatient treatment or detox centers.

1. **They should have a clear operational definition.**

Before choosing a recovery residence, find out what level of care is being offered. The NARR has set forth different levels of care ranging from non-clinical recovery housing (your typical sober home) to residences that offer clinical treatment (which means they should be licensed by the state). The owners or operators of the recovery residence should certainly know about these levels and in which category they fit. Refer to the table below for the NARR levels to learn what you should ask for, and what to expect:

NARR Level 1 (e.g., Oxford Houses)	
Typical Resident	Self-identifies as in recovery, some long-term, with peer-community accountability
On-Site Staffing	No on-site paid staff, peer-to-peer support
Governance	Democratically run
On-Site Supports	On-site peer support and off-site mutual support groups and, as needed, outside clinical services

NARR Level 2 (e.g., sober living homes)	
Typical Resident	Stable recovery but wish to have a more structured, peer-accountable and supportive living environment
On-Site Staffing	Resident house manager(s) often compensated by free or reduced fees
Governance	Residents participate in governance in concert with staff/recovery residence operator
On-Site Supports	Community/house meetings, peer recovery supports including "buddy systems," outside mutual support groups and clinical services are available and encouraged

NARR Level 3	
Typical Resident	Those who wish to have moderately structured daily schedule and life skills supports
On-Site Staffing	Paid house manager, administrative support, certified peer recovery support service provider

Governance	Resident participation varies; senior residents participate in residence-management decisions; depending on the state, may be licensed; peer recovery support staff are supervised
On-Site Supports	Community/house meetings, peer recovery supports including "buddy systems." Linked with mutual support groups and clinical services in the community, peer or professional life skills training on-site, peer recovery support services

NARR Level 4 (e.g., therapeutic community)	
Typical Resident	Require clinical oversight or monitoring, stays in these settings are typically briefer than in other levels
On-Site Staffing	Paid, licensed/credentialed staff and administrative support
Governance	Resident participation varies, organization authority hierarchy, clinical supervision
On-Site Supports	On-site clinical services, on-site mutual support group meetings, life skills training, peer recovery support services

2. **They should recognize that a substance use disorder is a chronic condition requiring a range of recovery supports.**

SAMHSA's principles maintain that recovery houses are uniquely qualified to assist individuals in all phases of recovery, especially those in early recovery (i.e., in the first twelve months) by furnishing social capital and recovery supports. This means that your recovery residence needs to provide or feed into a support network "comprising friends and family who are not abusing substances, peers with lived experience, trained recovery housing staff, clinical support, and access to community resources." Thus, the lure of warm-weather tourist destinations may entice those seeking a recovery vacation, but residences far away from family, positive friendships, and other support networks can undermine this important treatment principle.

3. **They should recognize that co-occurring mental disorders often accompany substance use disorders.**

According to SAMHSA's 2022 National Survey on Drug Use and Health, 21.5 million adults live with a co-occurring mental health and substance use disorder, including more than 15 percent of young adults aged eighteen to twenty-five.[193] This is why SAMHSA recommends that the operators and staff of recovery residences should be knowledgeable about how co-occurring disorders and resulting symptoms can increase a person's susceptibility for relapse.

4. **They should assess the needs of potential residents and whether the home is appropriate to meet these needs.**

According to SAMHSA, the following should be considered to determine the most appropriate residential setting:

- Level of care: the type, nature, and intensity of therapeutic services and recovery supports provided; ability to address specific needs

- Utilization of certified or appropriately trained peers with relevant lived experience

- Geographic area, neighborhood, or external surrounding environment of the recovery house

- Physical living environment

- Current residents: welcoming, committed to sobriety—are they mostly employed, supportive of one another?

- Medication-assisted treatment (MAT): does the operator or other house staff support the use of MAT, is the use of this medication properly monitored, are the other residents in the house also supportive of MAT, and are peers with MAT experience available for residents with severe opioid use disorder?

- Level of training and professionalism of house staff (e.g., co-occurring disorders, crisis interventions)

- Reputation regarding ethical business practices, including fraud and abuse of residents

- Relapse policy

- Availability of opioid overdose reversal drugs

5. **They should promote and use evidence-based practices such as MAT.**

Combining MAT with counseling has been proven effective in treating an opioid use disorder. SAMHSA guidelines promote MAT in conjunction with behavioral therapies, including the use of peer recovery coaches. Keep in mind that many recovery residences provide no clinical treatment (as the chart under Guideline #1 shows), but that alone shouldn't disqualify a sober home from consideration. Many successful homes in NARR's Level 1 and 2 categories, such as Oxford Houses, follow evidence-based practices and fit the individualized needs of their residents without medical services.

6. **They should have written policies, procedures, and resident expectations.**

It is a red flag when a sober home lacks even a basic document that sets forth its ground rules. SAMHSA recommends that a house staff member or designated peer clearly explain the house's standard operating procedures to every new resident and recommends that the resident should sign the documents and be provided a copy. These simple steps are rarely, if ever, found in the rogue sober homes that Aronberg and Padich investigate. If your prospective recovery residence can't follow this easy SAMHSA guideline, we recommend looking elsewhere.

7. **They should ensure quality, integrity, and resident safety.**

Every recovery residence, both good and bad, will promise to honor this principle, but it needs to be more than lip service. Specifically, SAMHSA recommends avoiding any recovery residence that engages in patient brokering (aka The Florida Shuffle). One way to decipher the ethics of a potential home is to find out whether it is certified or accredited under state law. State laws in this area differ widely across the country. In Florida, the NARR affiliate is FARR, which is the state-designated organization that provides voluntary certification of sober homes.

Since federal law continues to prevent local and state governments from requiring mandatory certification, registration, or accreditation of sober homes,[194] Aronberg's Sober Homes Task Force convinced the Florida legislature to enact legislation that requires FARR certification of all recovery residences that refer patients to treatment centers or receive such referrals. It's a carrot-and-stick approach: homes and treatment centers can get the referrals (as long as there are no kickbacks), but now the residences must be FARR-certified to do so.

FARR posts an updated list of all certified recovery residences on its website, along with their levels of care.[195] To obtain FARR certification, recovery residences must first fill out a comprehensive disclosure form of all owners, employees and affiliates, level of care, number of beds, MAT acceptance, fee schedule, and a host of other items. FARR then conducts an on-site inspection and mandates "unrestricted access to interview management, staff, and residents to ensure that policies, procedures and protocols are, in fact, implemented in the residential setting." The FARR staff assesses compliance with NARR standards "to ensure the residence offers safe, dignified, alcohol and drug-free, recovery supportive housing that blends into the surrounding community."[196]

The oversight does not end after FARR certification is achieved. Certified homes are subject to inspections without advance notice to ensure continued compliance with NARR standards.[197]

8. **They should learn and practice cultural competence.**

Since the disease of addiction does not discriminate, SAMHSA recommends that the staff of recovery residences should have training to "deal with individuals on a personal basis and respect different beliefs and backgrounds."

9. **They should maintain ongoing communication with interested parties and care specialists.**

As long as there is a signed release of confidential information, communication with a resident's loved ones, treatment providers, peer recovery specialists, and certain others can be a huge benefit. Successful recovery residences will embrace communication and avoid isolation, sharing information on the resident's progress, attendance, employment status, discharge planning, and other relevant topics among stakeholders to improve the quality of care.

10. **They should evaluate program effectiveness and resident success.**

Choose a recovery residence that is always evaluating itself, collecting data on measures such as abstinence from use, relapse rates, employment, and criminal justice involvement. Ask the recovery residence operator or staff for this information. Not only can you gain valuable insight into the home, but you can draw your own conclusions by how the recovery residence reacts to your probing questions. Don't be bashful when it comes to the recovery of your loved one: treat it like any other important healthcare decision.

When Aronberg led one of the first investigations into Purdue Pharma's marketing practices years ago, he never could have predicted the enormous death toll and societal costs of what would become an unprecedented opioid epidemic. When Campbell's brother was found dead in the same bedroom a young Dave Campbell lived in for eighteen years in Palm Beach County, the seasoned physician already understood how badly the world stigmatized those suffering from substance use disorders. Campbell's kid brother lived the stigma and died alone, with only his trusty dog by his side.

There are many quality healthcare providers, counselors, educational websites, and compassionate friends and family who can help. Never stop trying to find answers. Never stop working toward being part of the solution for this uniquely American crisis. Just as the opioid epidemic was not inevitable, its continued existence is not inevitable if enough of us do something about it.

CHAPTER 14

JERRY

Long before Aronberg and Campbell met, both had developed experience in fighting the opioid crisis. For Campbell, it was more than professional; it was personal. It was coping with a brother's decades of struggle while trying to maintain a loving fraternal relationship. For the landlubber surgeon, some of the best times of bonding occurred while at sea.

"Hey Jerry, snatch that line!" David Campbell yelled over the noise of the engine, the howling wind, the slapping of waves against the hull, and the ever-present sound of Coast Guard members and commercial fishers speaking over the marine radio.

"Got it, bro! She's a sixty-pounder!" replied the six-foot-two, broad-shouldered commercial fisherman known by his fishing buddies as "Scrambled." Jerry swung his 250-pound, brawny frame toward the electric fishing reel mounted on the gunwale. David Campbell, meanwhile, fished with a typical rod and reel. Jerry's electric reel was above his pay grade, as David fished for pleasure while his brother fished for work.

The gnarly thirty-foot, weather-beaten, single-screw commercial fishing vessel named "Miss Sheila" pitched from side-to-side in the turbulent Gulf Stream flowing off the coast of Palm Beach. A short and heavy fiberglass tool built for catch and not release, the rod bent toward the stern. Even the largest fish didn't have much of a chance. The aches and pains of Jerry's grueling occupation were suppressed for the time being as molecules of oxycodone attached to his brain's reward system. The pain medication had been prescribed by a reputable pain management group in the county.

That fishing trip was more than twenty years ago, just after the Sackler family and their company, Purdue Pharma, unleashed OxyContin on physicians in South Florida. As the years passed, their trips to sea became less frequent and their fraternal relationship became increasingly strained. In hindsight, David should have realized that Jerry's compulsions and cravings from his opioid and alcohol addiction were a more severe culprit than he recognized at the time.

One brother was a surgeon tasked with saving human lives and restoring function to disabled body parts, and the other a commercial fisherman tasked with butchering fish and providing food for his fellow Americans, rich and poor alike. Everyone needs a physician eventually, and everyone needs to eat. The brothers did not perceive any difference in their value for society. They were, after all, brothers with shared parents and grandparents. They were more alike than different, or so they liked to think.

Jerry was home on the sea. He flexed his knees for balance as the boat tossed and shifted in the six-foot swells, intensified by the Gulf Stream's northward-moving current. Shortly before, Jerry had downed an oxycodone tablet "just to be sure." Jerry's pain management physicians considered him a chronic pain patient who needed long-term opioid therapy, so there was no end in sight to his ubiquitous prescriptions. The gradual transition from a patient with an emerging opioid tolerance, to developing a substance use disorder, to becoming a full-fledged addict was like a runaway train that could not be stopped or slowed.

Jerry smiled as a wave nearly tossed his brother overboard. It was South Florida, the water was warm, and David could swim. He knew from experience that serious injury or drowning would not happen. Jerry thought, *I must bring David out more often—this is entertaining!*

Life on the open ocean had trained Jerry's sense of balance. He had his sea legs. Alcohol had not yet caused neuropathy with its trademarked numbness. That would have to wait. The fisherman was more comfortable in six-to-eight-foot swells, with the wind to his back, than rocking on his porch while sipping sweet tea.

David hung on for dear life, struggling to keep his inner-ear vestibular structure from swaying too many times. *If only I had had remembered to take Dramamine, or to stick a scopolamine patch behind my ear,* he thought. Sensing what his older brother was thinking, Jerry yelled over the cacophony of engine, waves, and wind, "Too late now, bro!"

While the brothers were tough on the outside, both had inherited the traits of empathy, compassion, resilience, and resolve from their parents, Kitty and Sloan. Neither enjoyed seeing the other physically sick or injured, or worse yet, with behavioral health conditions that, for Jerry, included recurrent and relapsing battles with depression, anxiety, emotional distress, and substance use disorders. As kids, neither could have predicted how drugs and alcohol would eventually tear down the walls of resilience. To this day, David remains saddened by the ineffectiveness of his feeble attempts to reverse the tragic course of his brother's life. Every day he tells himself that he should have done more and done it sooner. He was, after all, a trained physician. He should have been clear-eyed as a doctor. But he was blinded by fraternal bonds and machismo behaviors so common in Clan Campbell.

There were obvious physical similarities between these two Campbell brothers, more so than with the oldest, Ted. High cheekbones, droopy hound dog eyelids, ruddy Irish-Scottish-German chronically sunburned skin, and legs the size of logs, better built for a lumberjack than for a surgeon and a fisherman. As Jerry's addictions progressed, it became apparent that a key difference existed between them. It was a nebulous and ill-defined distinction at first, one that allowed the younger brother to develop severe substance use disorders while the others did not. It was a difference in part environmental and in part genetic. Nature and nurture combined to make different adults, even though they shared common parents and a common upbringing.

They shared an "Andy of Mayberry" youth with the austerity that comes from a working-class family in the town of Greenacres. Their father was the chief of police. The three brothers shared a small bedroom, where it was tight, but they did not know any difference. An antique oscillating fan was the only relief they got from the stifling South Florida heat. School was within walking distance and friends were everywhere. The bucolic setting included woods, fields, and canals full of catfish to eat and alligators to avoid. The town library was only a block away, next to the Little League field. Greenacres was as safe and satisfying a place to grow up as anywhere in the country. Back then, it was unforeseeable and unfathomable that Jerry would one day overdose on his cancer-riddled fentanyl while she was in the hospital fighting for her life after cancer surgery in Miami.

Jerry's right hand caressed the reel, as his left activated the electric switch. It was a delicate balance between too much or too little tension on the line. Deep water fish were prone to spit the hook if constant tension was not maintained on the monofilament line. Without warning, a massive wave hit the hull of Miss Sheila on her starboard side. The sound was sickening, as thousands of pounds of ocean water threatened the integrity of the aging fiberglass. She held, but the men on board did not. The impact of the wave threw them onto the slimy, bloody deck. In an instant, tangles of legs, backs, and butts converged in fish guts and seawater. Curse words filled the air. Jerry's oxycodone-saturated brain was no match for the abrupt pain caused by the trauma. The electric reel was wrenched from Jerry's grip. With nothing to hold on to, his body twisted into a pretzel, straining his back. It was not his first low back injury, nor his last.

The impact of the rogue wave smashed David's delicate surgeon's hands against the massive ice-filled fish box straddling the middle of the boat. He surveyed the damage to his digits and knew the injuries were minor. He admired his younger brother's resilience as Jerry rolled to his feet and, with a sweep of his outstretched hand, grabbed the still-bent fishing rod. It was as if his life depended on it. It did, to some extent. Sixty pounds of uncleaned, iced-down, kingfish might bring almost $100 at Pinder's fish market, enough money to buy groceries.

The reel had switched off at impact. With one hand on the rod, Jerry flipped the switch back on, and the electric motor hummed back to life. It was a comforting experience for David to hear the drone of the inboard gasoline engine and exhaust system vibrating at incompatible frequencies, competing with the sound of crashing waves and his younger brother's seaworn grunts.

"Stand back, bro! We can't have those girly surgeon hands of yours scuffed-up," Jerry jested. Underneath the tough outer veneer, the brothers shared a deep respect for each other. The surgeon understood the harsh life of his brother. The fisherman respected the many years of school and studying it took for his older brother to become a surgeon. They also shared a work ethic handed down from their father, Sloan, who was never one to shirk his responsibilities. He showed his three children that work was part of life. Complaining was not an option. There was always a side job he could hand off to one of his boys to help put food on the table. In David's family back then, before he had children of his own, the expectation was everyone had to make their way in school, sports, and work. You chose your own destiny but could always rely on a helping hand when needed.

Jerry's physicians treated his pain with a regimen of long-acting opioid pain medicine. They also prescribed him short-acting pills for breakthrough pain before it was time for another long-acting pill. For Jerry, that meant taking both OxyContin and Percocet. As the opioid crisis grew in the United States, so did the severity of Jerry's opioid use disorder and so did his willingness to buy and barter pills on the illicit market.

Jerry earned the moniker "Scrambled" the hard way. Drugs, alcohol, and a learning disability made him a target for abuse, even by his friends. But he had to work, so he endured the emotional pain. It hurt him in ways he would never admit, to be treated with such callous disregard for his emotions by those he was forced, by the necessity of work, to call his friends. It wasn't the cruel words that killed Jerry, although their corrosive effect on his psyche eroded the foundation of resilience built by his parents. It was the potent synthetic opioid, fentanyl, that was Jerry's ultimate undoing.

David felt inept at determining how to help his younger brother. He encouraged and facilitated many rounds of outpatient treatment coordinated with Jerry's pain management and medical team. Yet, he could not convince Jerry to stop excessive alcohol consumption, and he could not effectively explain to his younger brother the dramatic risk of mouth and throat cancer from chewing tobacco, judging by the fact that Jerry would have been unrecognizable without a bulbous protrusion of his cheek caused by the wad packed between his lower lip and gums. He could not make his younger brother's physicians know his brother like he knew him, as the sensitive, caring, and compassionate human he was with a mind addled by alcohol, a learning disability from birth, and a body the size of a refrigerator. To his treating physicians, he was a patient with many overlapping medical co-morbidities that warranted treatment.

As Purdue Pharma and its pharmaceutical marketing team flooded the United States with misinformation about the addictive potential of its blockbuster pain pill, thousands of patients like Jerry were placed on daily opioid therapy for chronic,

non-cancer pain. As with so many others, Jerry was never ta-
pered, discontinued, or discharged. He also never overdosed.
That is, not until the end, when his first overdose was his last.

David knows that his brother bore responsibility for choices
he made as a young man, before he was addicted to drugs. But
as OxyContin swept the country, the long-term opioid therapy
he was prescribed for chronic pain was more than he could
withstand. Jerry did not choose to become addicted to opioids.
His pain management physicians never expected him to become
addicted either. His unique genetic makeup, combined with his
environment, fostered his addiction. Eventually, the opioids hijacked his brain. Brain fog, dopesickness, and cravings were a
daily burden.

Shame, stigma, and bias hung like a cloud over Jerry's final
years. One at a time, his fishing buddies stopped coming to the
dock for a visit. His aunts, uncles, and cousins stayed away unless
there was an emergency. Jerry grew increasingly despondent, and
his anxiety and depression led to additional drug and alcohol
use, which in turn led to more maladaptive behaviors, burned
emotional bridges, and frequent bizarre thought patterns. Still,
Jerry remained a part of the tight-knit Campbell nuclear family,
which remained loyal to the end and turned the other cheek every time he acted poorly. When Jerry acted the fool while high
or clawed into his mother's supply of pain medication used to
treat her terminal cancer, his family scolded, tried to help, but
ultimately took him back into the fold. They assisted with Jerry's
insurance premiums and put food on the table for his wife and
son. He was never homeless. Several people outside the family
chastised the Campbells for helping Jerry when he was down

and out, accusing them of enabling Jerry's addiction. In so doing, the callous, judgmental outsiders who urged David's family to abandon his sibling in need were ignoring the realities known to experts in the field of addiction medicine. Jerry was sick with a brain disease, not a moral failing.

On a lonely, isolated night in 2016, Jerry was house-sitting at his parents' home while his mother was in Miami recovering from cancer surgery. His father, a devoted and doting husband, was at her bedside. The former chief of police was no fool. He knew that his addicted son would turn the house upside down looking for his mother's stash of pain medicine. So, the Chief had taken all the medications with him to Miami—or so he thought.

As expected, Jerry was craving opioids. His heart probably skipped a beat when he came across a Ziploc bag full of fentanyl transdermal patches meant for his mother when she returned home to recuperate. The Chief had somehow overlooked the supply hidden in his wife's lingerie drawer. The coroner later documented several articles of his mother's clothing slung across the room with half-opened fentanyl patches littering the floor next to Jerry's rigid body, in rigor mortis. His cravings and compulsive behavior, without regard for the consequences, marked his final actions as someone with a severe opioid use disorder. Many people with opioid use disorder describe that just "feeling not sick" is each day's primary goal. Jerry did not want to get high. Rather, he did not want to feel dopesick.

During his last few minutes alive, Kitty Campbell, his mother, lay in a hospital bed with her devoted husband of sixty years, the Chief, by her side. For the five years since her mouth and throat cancer had spread, she was expected to die first in the family.

With terminal cancer ravaging her body, her three grown children still too young to collect Social Security, and her husband fit as a fiddle, there was never a question about who would go first. Jerry proved that night how life has a way of throwing curveballs.

After years of diligently hiding all drugs from Jerry, Chief Campbell had slipped up just that one time, which is all that it took. That oversight weighed heavily on him, a man who wrongly blamed himself for his son's overdose. In the hectic hours leading up to the trip to Miami, he had to feed and walk the dog, clean the dishes, and pack Kitty's clothes and essential items and medications, along with an overnight bag for himself. No one knew how long she would be in the hospital this time. In fact, no one knew if she would even survive this surgery and hospitalization.

Jerry's trusty family dog, an old yellow Labrador retriever, stood guard and became vocal. A watchful neighbor heard the dog barking and came to check on the house. He became suspicious when Jerry did not answer the door. Greenacres is a small town, and the Chief never locked his doors, knowing that no one would be foolish enough to break into his house. The neighbor let himself in and immediately found Jerry dead in bed and called the police. The loyal Lab never left Jerry's side until Chief Campbell arrived home an hour later from Miami. Campbell's father said identifying his youngest son's body was the most horrific thing he'd ever had to face.

The detective that searched the room where Jerry was found dead discovered the discarded fentanyl patches, various scattered pill bottles, and even an opened and half-empty bottle of vodka. The medical examiner's autopsy and chemical toxicology screening revealed several potentially lethal drugs and chemicals in

Jerry's body, including medications taken during the same day for high blood pressure, diabetes, and heart disease. But the medical examiner concluded that Jerry's death, like so many victims of the Florida Shuffle, was due primarily to fentanyl, with the fatal dose of medication too easily diverted from its intended patient.

Humans are sentimental by nature, and each unexpected and unnecessary death can create a lifetime of sorrow. Scores of needless deaths can spark a movement for change, which has been our intent in presenting the stories of those caught in the grip of an unprecedented man-made epidemic followed by a vicious cycle of exploitation. Jerry avoided the Florida Shuffle but not the opioids aggressively and disingenuously pushed by Purdue Pharma onto doctors and their patients as a miracle cure for pain with minimal risk of addiction.

That same day, around 116 people died from an opioid over-dose in the United States.[198] Each one may seem like a small drop in a bucket to some, a cold statistic to others. For family and loved ones, it is a tragedy beyond words, often following a long, arduous journey of addiction and all the troubling behaviors it spawns. For the ignorant or heartless who perpetuate the stigma of addiction, Jerry's death, like the others, will be rationalized as the inevitable demise of someone who chose to play Russian roulette. But the driving force behind the Sober Homes Task Force and all the advocates, families, and behavioral health profession-als who dedicate their lives to rescuing those still living with this devastating brain disease is the common understanding that all lives are worth saving. A society can be judged on how it treats its most vulnerable citizens, and how we care for those ravaged by addiction or victimized by the Florida Shuffle reveals more about us than about them.

In Jerry's final moments, his brain must have welcomed the surge of euphoria as the potent psychoactive chemical coursed through his bloodstream and bound to the opioid receptors in his brain. He had felt the surge many times before. It was the "dragon" that he and the others addicted to opioids searched for with obsessive, compulsive, and reckless abandon. Jerry knew that his irrational behavior was dangerous. Even in 2016, fentanyl supplies were increasing in the illicit drug market in Florida. David told his brother many times to always have someone nearby if he was using any controlled substance, legally or otherwise. Jerry knew that the opioid overdose reversal agent, naloxone, cannot be given to yourself if you become unconscious. But knowledge and behaviors are often out of sync with those suffering from substance use disorder.

Although the medical examiner determined that fentanyl caused Jerry's death, his family attributed his demise to all the tough times and desperate circumstances he endured in his fifty-four years of life. His death left a grieving and broken family to pick up the pieces and move on.

Jerry was sick, but was also empathetic, compassionate, and kind. He is universally missed by his fellow commercial grunts, even those who called him Scrambled, and that was all of them. One thing is certain: If Jerry were alive and healthy enough today, he would be off the coast of Palm Beach cursing at the waves, dipping Copenhagen, and winching in fish-after-fish. That is his legacy. That is how David Campbell chooses to remember his kid brother.

ACKNOWLEDGEMENTS

This book would not have been possible without the help of the extremely talented, devoted, and understanding team members at Indigo River Publishing, who work diligently to prepare the best publications possible for their readers—and make these messages of hope, and the legacy of those lost in the opioid epidemic, available to everyone.

We are especially grateful to Deborah Froese, executive editor for Indigo River Publishing, Marci Carson, our lead editor, who took a dual-authored book penned by two busy individuals in their separate professions and gave it a voice, and Linda Dessau, our copy editor.

We are extra grateful to Chris Jacobsen, who sadly passed away after having spoken with Dr. Dave Campbell for hour upon hour, and working with Dave Aronberg's team members for weeks during the search for his missing daughter, Jenna, before and after her remains were discovered. Chris loved his daughter dearly and left a lasting impression upon the veteran investigators who marveled at his tenacity. May Chris and Jenna both be of blessed memory, and may Jenna's murder be solved.

We are also grateful to the many people who have had their stories told in this book, who generously gave their time to provide extensive interviews with Dr. Campbell and had conversations with Dave Aronberg. Many of their names have been changed to protect them from stigma and reprisals. Although the Florida Shuffle has been largely eradicated in Palm Beach County, it continues to thrive elsewhere.

– Dave Aronberg & Dr. Dave Campbell

SELECTED BIBLIOGRAPHY

Campbell, Dr. Dave. *The Teen Formula: A Parent's Guide to Helping Your Child Avoid Substance Abuse.* CreateSpace Independent Publishing, 2017.

Macy, Beth. *Dopesick: Dealers, Doctors, and the Drug Company that Addicted America.* Boston: Little, Brown and Company, 2018.

Quinones, Sam. *Dreamland: The True Tale of America's Opiate Epidemic.* London: Bloomsbury USA, 2015.

Quinones, Sam. *The Least of Us: True Tales of America and Hope in the Time of Fentanyl and Meth.* London: Bloomsbury USA, 2021.

REFERENCES

1   "Injury Facts, Odds of Dying," National Safety Council, 2021, https:// injuryfacts.nsc.org/all-injuries/preventable-death-overview/odds-of-dying/; Tim Henderson, "Death Rates for People Under 40 Have Skyrocketed. Blame Fentanyl," *Missouri Independent*, September 5, 2023, https://missouriindependent.com/2023/09/05/death-rates-for-people-under-40-have-skyrocketed-blame-fentanyl/; Nusalba Mizan, "Fact-Check: Is Fentanyl the Leading Cause of Death Among American Adults?" *Austin American-Statesman*, October 2, 2022, https://www.statesman.com/story/news/politics/politifact/2022/10/02/fact-check-fentanyl-leading-cause-of-death-among-adults/65417990007/.

2   Alan Johnson (Chief Assistant State Attorney), interview by Campbell, June 2022. Johnson cited an Optum Insurance Company study from 2015.

3   John LaRosa, "$42 Billion U.S. Addiction Rehab Industry Poised for Growth, and Challenges," *Market Research.com*, February 5, 2020, https:// blog.marketresearch.com/42-billion-u.s.-addiction-rehab-industry-poised-for-growth-and-challenges.

4   Christina Andrews et al., "Despite Resources From the ACA, Most States Do Little to Help Addiction Treatment Programs Implement Health Care Reform, *Health Affairs (Millwood)* 34, no. 5 (May 2015): 828–35, https://www. ncbi.nlm.nih.gov/pmc/articles/PMC4706741/

5   Lawrence Mower, "'Kenny Chatman Kidnapped Me.' Read One Woman's Human Trafficking Story," *The Palm Beach Post*, May 16, 2017.

6   Mower, "Chatman Kidnapped Me."

7   Mower, "Chatman Kidnapped Me."

8   Mower, "Chatman Kidnapped Me."

9   Mower, "Chatman Kidnapped Me."

10   Mower, "Chatman Kidnapped Me."

11   Mower, "Chatman Kidnapped Me."

12   Mower, "Chatman Kidnapped Me."

13   Jane Musgrave, "Notorious Treatment Center Operator Chatman Gets 27 Years in Prison," *The Palm Beach Post*, July 31, 2017, https://www.palmbeachpost.com/news/20170517/notorious-treatment-center-operator-chatman-gets-27-years-in-prison.

14   Musgrave, "Notorious."

15   Ken Daniels, telephone conversation with Dave Aronberg, May 1, 2023.

16   Lisa Daniels-Goldman, telephone conversation with Dave Aronberg, August 1, 2023; Craig Custance, "Red Wings Announcer Ken Daniels Shares His Heartbreaking Loss to Save Others From Predatory Rehabs," *The Athletic*, November 13, 2017, https://theathletic.com/154171/2017/11/13/red-wings-announcer-ken-daniels-shares-his-heartbreaking-loss-to-save-others-from-predatory-rehabs/.

17   Lisa Daniels-Goldman, Aug 1, 2023.

18   Lisa Daniels-Goldman, Aug 1, 2023.

19   Custance, "Ken Daniels."

20   Custance, "Ken Daniels."

21   Lisa Daniels-Goldman, telephone conversation with Dave Aronberg, May 1, 2023.

22   Custance, "Ken Daniels."

23   Lisa Daniels-Goldman, "Jamie's Story," Jamie Daniels Foundation, 2023, https://jamiedanielsfoundation.org/jamies-story/.

24   Custance, "Ken Daniels."

25   Custance, "Ken Daniels."

26   Custance, "Ken Daniels."

27   Custance, "Ken Daniels."

28   Lisa Daniels-Goldman, Jamie Daniels Foundation, 2023, https://jamie-danielsfoundation.org/.

29   Lisa Daniels-Goldman, Aug 1, 2023.

30   Ken Daniels, May 1, 2023.

31   Lisa Daniels-Goldman, "What We Do."

32   Carol Cain, "After Son's Death, Red Wings Announcer Ken Daniels Joins Opioid Fight," Detroit Free Press, June 18, 2018, https://www.freep.com/story/money/business/columnists/carol-cain/2018/04/14/ken-daniels-detroit-red-wings-opioids/513794002/.

33   Brad Emons, "Red Wings Broadcaster Ken Daniels Shares About Tragic Death of Son From Opioid Overdose," Hometown Life, December 3, 2017, https://www.hometownlife.com/story/sports/hockey/2017/12/01/wings-broadcaster-ken-daniels-talks-tragic-loss-his-son-opioid-overdose-novi-high-school/910178001/.

34   ESPN E60 (@E60), "The story of @DetroitRedWings play-by-play commentator Ken Daniels, and the drug scam that led to the tragic death of his son", April 15, 2018, https://twitter.com/E60/status/982038150137696256.

35   "Henry M. Flagler in Florida Timeline," Historical Society of Palm Beach County, accessed April 17, 2020, https://pbchistory.org/flagler-era-through-boom-to-bust/.

36   David Armstrong, "The Family Trying to Escape Blame for the Opioid Crisis," The Atlantic, April 10, 2018, https://www.theatlantic.com/health/archive/2018/04/sacklers-oxycontin-opioids/557525/.

37   Patrick Radden Keefe, "The Family That Built an Empire of Pain," The New Yorker, October 23, 2017, https://www.newyorker.com/magazine/2017/10/30/the-family-that-built-an-empire-of-pain.

38   Armstrong, "The Family Trying."

39   Jane Porter and Hershel Jick, "Addiction Rare in Patients Treated with Narcotics," letter to the editor, The New England Journal of Medicine 302, no. 2 (January 10, 1980), https://www.nejm.org/doi/full/10.1056/NEJM198001103020221.

40   Sarah Zhang, "The One-Paragraph Letter From 1980 That Fueled the

Opioid Crisis," *The Atlantic*, June 2, 2017, https://www.theatlantic.com/health/archive/2017/06/nejm-letter-opioids/528840/.

41   Marilynn Marchione, "Painful Words: How a 1980 Letter Fueled the Opioid Epidemic," *STAT*, May 31, 2017, https://www.statnews.com/2017/05/31/opioid-epidemic-nejm-letter/.

42   Pamela T.M. Leung et al., "A 1980 Letter on the Risk of Opioid Addiction," letter to the editor, *The New England Journal of Medicine* 376, no. 22, June 1, 2017, https://www.nejm.org/doi/full/10.1056/NEJMc1700150.

43   Pat Beall, "Purdue Pharma Plants the Seeds of the Opioid Epidemic in a Tiny Virginia Town and Others," *The Palm Beach Post*, accessed. July 17, 2023, https://heroin.palmbeachpost.com/purdue-pharma-plants-seeds-of-opioid-epidemic/.

44   Beall, "Purdue Pharma."

45   The Joint Commission, "Pain Assessment and Management Standards for Joint Commission Accredited Health Care Organizations," February 2020, https://www.jointcommission.org/-/media/tjc/documents/corporate-communication/pain-management-standards-and-responses-to-myths-final-feb-2020.pdf.

46   Joint Commission, "Pain."

47   Joint Commission, "Pain."

48   Miles Gart, "Pain is Not the Fifth Vital Sign," *Medical Economics*, May 20, 2017, https://www.medicaleconomics.com/view/pain-not-fifth-vital-sign.

49   Brian Zimmerman, "7 Things to Know About the History of The Joint Commission Pain Standards," *Becker's Hospital Review*, February 28, 2017, https://www.beckershospitalreview.com/opioids/7-things-to-know-about-the-history-of-the-joint-commission-pain-standards.html.

50   Barry Meier and Eric Lipton, "Under Attack, Drug Maker Turned to Giuliani for Help," *New York Times, December 28, 2007*, https://www.nytimes.com/2007/12/28/us/politics/28oxycontin.html.

51   Caitlin Esch, "How One Sentence Helped Set off the Opioid Crisis," Marketplace podcast, The Uncertain Hour, December 13, 2017, https://www.marketplace.org/2017/12/13/opioid/.

52   Harriet Ryan, Lisa Girion, and Scott Glover, "'You Want a Description of Hell?' OxyContin's 12-Hour Problem," *Los Angeles Times,* May 5, 2016, https://www.latimes.com/projects/oxycontin-part1/.

53   Ryan, Girion, and Glover, "Hell."

54   U.S. Food and Drug Administration, "NDA 020553/S-002 Approval Letter," December 9, 1996, https://www.accessdata.fda.gov/drugsatfda_docs/nda/96/020553s002.pdf.

55   Richard J. Pacheco, "The Use and Misuse of OxyContin," third-year paper, Harvard Law School, 2002, https://dash.harvard.edu/bitstream/handle/1/8846740/Pacheco.pdf?sequence=1&isAllowed=y.

56   Esch, "One Sentence."

57   Andrew Kolodny, "How FDA Failures Contributed to the Opioid Crisis," *AMA Journal of Ethics* 22, no. 8 (August 2020): 743–750, https://journalofethics.ama-assn.org/article/how-fda-failures-contributed-opioid-crisis/2020-08.

58   Andrew Kolodny, telephone conversation with Dave Aronberg, January 23, 2024.

59   United States Government Accountability Office, "Prescription Drugs: OxyContin Abuse and Diversion and Efforts to Address the Problem," GAO-04-110 (Washington, DC: December 2003), https://www.gao.gov/assets/a240885.html.

60   Federal Bureau of Investigation, "Willie Sutton," FBI, accessed July 17, 2023, https://www.fbi.gov/history/famous-cases/willie-sutton.

61   Substance Abuse and Mental Health Services Administration (SAMHSA), "Why Addiction is a 'Disease,' and Why It's Important," resource guide, accessed July 17, 2023, https://www.samhsa.gov/sites/default/files/programs_campaigns/02._webcast_2_resources.pdf.

62   Alan Johnson, interview by Dr. Dave Campbell, May 2, 2022.

63   Alan Johnson, May 2, 2022.

64   Alan Johnson, May 2, 2022.

65   Ted Padich, interview by Dr. Dave Campbell, February 12, 2022.

66   Ted Padich, February 12, 2022.

67   Alan Johnson, May 2, 2022.

68   "Michael," telephone interview by Dr. Dave Campbell, May 2, 2022.

69   Michael, May 2, 2022.

70   Michael, May 2, 2022.

71   Michael, May 2, 2022.

72   Michael, May 2, 2022.

73   Michael, May 2, 2022.

74   Michael, May 2, 2022.

75   Michael, May 2, 2022.

76   Michael, May 2, 2022.

77   Michael, May 2, 2022.

78   Michael, May 2, 2022.

79   Michael, May 2, 2022.

80   Michael, May 2, 2022.

81   Michael, May 2, 2022.

82   Michael, May 2, 2022.

83   *Case 9:20-mj-08265-BER Document 8 FLSD Docket 7/30/2020* (United States District Court for the Southern District of Florida, justice.gov., p. 7, accessed 9/26/2020), https://www.justice.gov/criminal-vns/file/1312631/download.

84   "Case 9:20."

85   U.S. Government Accountability Office, "Prescription Drugs: OxyContin Abuse and Diversion and Efforts to Address the Problem," GAO-04-110 (Washington, D.C.: December 2003), https://www.gao.gov/assets/gao-04-110.pdf.

86   Michael J. Mooney, "Are There Really More Pain Clinics in Broward Than McDonald's?" *Broward Palm Beach News Times*, March 2, 2010, https://www.browardpalmbeach.com/news/are-there-really-more-pain-clinics-in-broward-than-mcdonalds-6451705.

87   Ryan, Girion, and Glover, "Hell."

88   Donald M. Goldenbaum et al., "Physicians Charged with Opioid Analgesic-Prescribing Offenses," *Pain Medicine 9, no. 6, (September 2008): 737–47,* https://doi.org/10.1111/j.1526-4637.2008.00482.x.

89   National Institute on Drug Abuse, "Heroin Use Is Driven by Its Low Cost and High Availability," January 1, 2018, https://www.drugabuse.gov/publications/research-reports/relationship-between-prescription-drug-abuse-heroin-use/heroin-use-driven-by-its-low-cost-high-availability/.

90   Sari Horwitz and Scott Higham, "The Flow of Fentanyl: In the Mail, Over the Border," *Washington Post,* August 23, 2019, https://www.washingtonpost.com/investigations/2019/08/23/fentanyl-flowed-through-us-postal-service-vehicles-crossing-southern-border/.

91   Fatima Hussein and Eric Tucker, "U.S. Announces Sweeping Action Against Chinese Fentanyl Supply Chain Producers," *Associated Press,* October 3, 2023, https://apnews.com/article/fentanyl-us-china-mexico-sanctions-drugs-c9ee14f171f1fcbd4db3452cd0bd1d90 .

92   National Institute on Drug Abuse, "Heroin Use."

93   Amy Keller, "Strongest Pain Pills," *DrugRehab.com,* accessed July 17, 2023, https://www.drugrehab.com/addiction/opioid-strength/.

94   United States Drug Enforcement Administration, "Fentanyl," fact sheet, accessed July 17, 2023, https://www.dea.gov/factsheets/fentanyl.

95   Palm Beach County Medical Examiner, 2023 Snapshot with 23 pending cases (February 2024).

96   Sarah DeWeerdt, "Tracing the US Opioid Crisis to Its Roots," *Nature,* September 11, 2019, https://www.nature.com/articles/d41586-019-02686-2.

97   Jen Christensen, "U.S. Life Expectancy is Still on the Decline. Here's Why," *CNN,* November 26, 2019, https://www.cnn.com/2019/11/26/health/us-life-expectancy-decline-study/index.html; "U.S. Life Expectancy 1950–2023," *Macrotrends,* 2023, https://www.macrotrends.net/countries/USA/united-states/life-expectancy.

98   CDC National Center for Health Statistics, "Life Expectancy in the U.S. Dropped for the Second Year in a Row in 2021," news release, August 31, 2022, https://www.cdc.gov/nchs/pressroom/nchs_press_releases/2022/20220831.htm.

99   FB Ahmad et al., "Provisional Drug Overdose Death Counts," CDC National Center for Health Statistics, 2023, https://www.cdc.gov/nchs/nvss/vsrr/drug-overdose-data.htm.

100   The White House, "Dr. Rahul Gupta Releases Statement on CDC's New Overdose Death Data," press release, January 11, 2023, https://www.whitehouse.gov/ondcp/briefing-room/2023/01/11/dr-rahul-gupta-releases-statement-on-cdcs-new-overdose-death-data-2/#_ftn1.

101   National Safety Council, "Addressing the Opioid Crisis," accessed July 18, 2023, https://www.nsc.org/community-safety/safety-topics/opioids/prescription-drug-misuse.

102   Jan Hoffman and Katie Benner, "Purdue Pharma Pleads Guilty to Criminal Charges for Opioid Sales," *New York Times*, October 21, 2020, https://www.nytimes.com/2020/10/21/health/purdue-opioids-criminal-charges.html#:~:text=The%20company%20pleaded%20guilty%20to,health%20records%20company%2C%20Practice%20Fusion.

103   Brian Mann and Martha Bebinger, "Purdue Pharma, Sacklers Reach $6 Billion Deal With State Attorneys General, *NPR*, March 3, 2022, https://www.npr.org/2022/03/03/1084163626/purdue-sacklers-oxycontin-settle-ment; Brian Mann, "Federal Judge Approves Landmark $8.3 Billion Purdue Pharma Opioid Settlement," *NPR*, November 17, 2020, https://www.npr.org/2020/11/17/936022386/federal-judge-approves-landmark-8-3-bil-lion-purdue-pharma-opioid-settlement; Dani Alexis Ryskamp, "Purdue Pharma Pleads Guilty, Reaching $8.3 Billion Settlement," *Expert Institute*, December 7, 2020, https://www.expertinstitute.com/resources/insights/purdue-pharma-pleads-guilty-reaching-8-3-billion-settlement/;   Purdue Pharma, "Confirmed Plan of Reorganization Facilitates Creation of New Company—"Knoa Pharma, press release, September 3, 2021, https://www.purduepharma.com/news/2021/09/03/confirmed-plan-of-reorganization-fa-cilitates-creation-of-new-company-knoa-pharma/.

104   Meryl Kornfield, "Sacklers Offer $1 Billion More Than Planned to Settle Thousands of Opioid Lawsuits," *Washington Post*, March 16, 2021, https://www.washingtonpost.com/business/2021/03/16/purdue-sackler-opioids-set-tlement/; Jan Hoffman, "Purdue Pharma is Dissolved and Sacklers Pay $4.5 Billion to Settle Opioid Claims," *New York Times*, September 1, 2021, https://www.nytimes.com/2021/09/01/health/purdue-sacklers-opioids-settlement.html.

105   Devan Cole and Ariane de Vogue, "Supreme Court Blocks $6 Billion Opioid Settlement That Would Have Given the Sackler Family Immunity," *CNN*, August 10, 2023, https://www.cnn.com/2023/08/10/politics/supreme-court-purdue-pharma-opioid-settlement/index.html; Abbie VanSickle, "Supreme Court Jeopardizes Opioid Deal, Rejecting Protections for Sacklers," *New York Times*, June 27, 2024, https://www.nytimes.com/2024/06/27/us/supreme-court-opioid-settlement.html.

106   *Harrington v. Purdue Pharma L.P.*, 603 U.S. ___ (2024), Docket No. 23-124, slip op. at 7, 18.

107   Beth Macy, *Dopesick* (New York: Hachette Book Group, 2018), 42.

108   *Case 9:20-mj-08265-BER Document 8 FLSD Docket 7/30/2020* (United States District Court for the Southern District of Florida, justice.gov., p. 7, accessed September 26, 2020), https://www.justice.gov/opa/press-release/file/1300031/download.

109   Substance Abuse and Mental Health Services Administration (SAMHSA), "Key Substance Use and Mental Health Indicators in the United States: Results From the 2022 National Survey on Drug Use and Health." 52, https://www.samhsa.gov/data/sites/default/files/reports/rpt42731/2022-nsduh-nnr.pdf.

110   *SAMHSA*, "Key Substance Use," 53.

111   Jeanette M. Tetrault and Ismene L. Petrakis, "Partnering with Psychiatry to Close the Education Gap: An Approach to the Addiction Epidemic, *Journal of General Internal Medicine* 32, no. 12 (December 107): 1387–89, https://www.ncbi.nlm.nih.gov/pmc/articles/PMC5698217/.

112   SAMHSA, "Key Indicators."

113   Partnership to End Addiction, "Addiction Medicine: Closing the Gap between Science and Practice," May 2012, last updated November 2023, https://drugfree.org/reports/addiction-medicine-closing-the-gap-between-science-and-practice/; B.P. Smyth et al., "Lapse and relapse following inpatient treatment of opiate dependence," *Irish Medical Journal* 103, no. 6 (June 2010), https://pubmed.ncbi.nlm.nih.gov/20669601/; National Institute on Drug Abuse, "Principles of Drug Addiction Treatment: A Research-Based Guide—Third Edition," January 2014, accessed July 17, 2023, https://archives.nida.nih.gov/sites/default/files/podat-3rdEd-508.pdf.

114   Lisa Riordan Seville, Anna Schecter, and Hannah Rappleye, "Florida's Billion-Dollar Drug Treatment Industry is Plagued by Overdoses, Fraud," *NBC News*, June 25, 2017, https://www.nbcnews.com/feature/megyn-kelly/florida-s-billion-dollar-drug-treatment-industry-plagued-overdoses-fraud-n773376.

115   *The 2022 Florida Statutes—including 2022 Special Session A and 2023 Special Session B* (leg.state.fl.us, Section 817.505(1)(a), Fla. Stat., Online Sunshine, 2022), http://www.leg.state.fl.us/Statutes/index.cfm?App_mode=Display_Statute&URL=0800-0899/0817/Sections/0817.505.html.

116   Custance, "Ken Daniels."

117   *Case 9:20-mj-08265-BER. Document 8. FLSD Docket 7/30/2020* (justice.gov, United States District Court for the Southern District of Florida. p. 7, https://www.justice.gov/criminal-vns/file/1312631/download.

118   Alan Johnson, interview by Dr. Dave Campbell, September 25, 2020.

119   Jane Gross, "In Florida, Addicts Find an Oasis of Sobriety," *New York Times*, November 16, 2007,. https://www.nytimes.com/2007/11/16/us/16recovery.html.

120   Lizette Alvarez, "Haven for Recovering Addicts Now Profits From Their Relapses," *New York Times*, June 20, 2017, https://www.nytimes.com/2017/06/20/us/delray-beach-addiction.html.

121   Proviso Group, "Minutes—Approved by Al Johnson," Office of the State Attorney, Fifteenth Judicial Circuit in and for Palm Beach County, July 12, 2016, https://sa15.org/.

122   Florida Medical Examiners Commission (2022).

123   Palm Beach County Fire Rescue (2023).

124   Ted Padich, interview by Dr. Dave Campbell, February 9, 2021.

125   Julius Whigham II, "Boca Raton Doctor Pleads Guilty to Insurance Fraud; Losses Said to Top $17 Million," *The Palm Beach Post*, July 13, 2021, https://www.palmbeachpost.com/story/news/crime/2021/07/13/boca-raton-doctor-pleads-guilty-insurance-fraud-sober-home-cases/7942167002/.

126   Alan Johnson, September 25, 2020.

127   Ryan Van Velzer, "Retired Palm Beach Sheriff's Deputy Accused of Patient Brokering," *Sun Sentinel*, March 27, 2017, https://www.sun-sentinel.com/local/palm-beach/fl-pn-retired-deputy-patient-brokering-20170321-story.html.

128   Julius Whigham II, "Former PBSO Deputy Sentenced to 5 Years for Patient Brokering, Charity Fraud," *The Palm Beach Post*, May 20, 2020, https://www.palmbeachpost.com/story/news/crime/2020/05/20/former-pbso-deputy-sentenced-to-5-years-for-patient-brokering-charity-fraud/112305026/.

129   *Probable Cause Affidavit for Robert Jean Simeone* (March 15, 2017).

130   Robert Jean Simeone.

131   Robert Jean Simeone.

132   Jane Musgrave, "Why Judge's Ruling on Patient Brokering May Up-End Prosecutions," *The Palm Beach Post*, February 7, 2019, https://www.palmbeachpost.com/story/news/crime/2019/02/06/why-judges-ruling-on-patient-brokering-may-up-end-prosecutions/5472685007/.

133   *State v. Kigar. 279 So. 3d 217* (Fla. Dist. Ct. App. 2019), https://casetext.com/case/state-v-kigar; Marc Freeman, "Ex-Deputy Admits Cheating Drug-Recovery Industry and Stealing From Children's Charity. He's Going to Prison for 5 Years," *Sun Sentinel*, May 19, 2020, https://www.sun-sentinel.com/local/palm-beach/fl-ne-robert-simeone-felonies-plea-deal-20200519-udoctr5ainakll2fzkwabx5bfq-story.html.

134   Marc Freeman, "Children of Wounded Soldiers Stiffed; Ex-Deputy Accused of Theft," *Sun Sentinel*, February 21, 2020, https://www.sun-sentinel.com/local/palm-beach/fl-ne-robert-simeone-new-theft-charges-20200222-ypmvprftyfagvke4hwj6jdwshu-story.html.

135   Freeman, "Ex-Deputy."

136   U.S. Department of Justice, "Florida Doctor Sentenced for Substance Abuse Treatment Fraud Scheme," press release, January 10, 2023, https://www.justice.gov/opa/pr/florida-doctor-sentenced-substance-abuse-treatment-fraud-scheme.

137   Hannah Phillips, "'Necessary Evil': Why Sober-Home Fraudster Michael Ligotti Will Get to Leave Prison Early," *The Palm Beach Post*, December 12, 2023, https://www.palmbeachpost.com/story/news/crime/2023/12/12/addiction-doctor-michael-ligottis-20-year-prison-sentence-cut-in-half/71823720007/.

138   *Probable Cause Affidavit for James Kigar* (October 19, 2016).

139   *The 2022 Florida Statutes—including 2022 Special Session A and 2023 Special Session B* (leg.state.fl.us, Section 817.505(1)(a), Fla. Stat., Online Sunshine, 2022), http://www.leg.state.fl.us/Statutes/index.cfm?App_mode=Display_Statute&URL=0800-0899/0817/Sections/0817.505.html.

140   Skyler Swisher and Ryan Van Velzer, "Two Arrested in Crackdown on Unscrupulous Drug-Treatment Providers, Authorities Say," *Sun Sentinel*, October 25, 2016, https://www.sun-sentinel.com/local/palm-beach/fl-sober-home-prosecutors-palm-20161025-story.html.

141   James Kigar.

142   James Kigar.

143   James Kigar.

144   James Kigar.

145   Freeman, "Ex-Deputy."

146   Janet K., "Whole Life Recovery," *The Real Yellow Pages*, online review, June 20, 2016, https://www.yellowpages.com/boynton-beach-fl/mip/whole-life-recovery-514726656#yp-rating.

147   Marc Freeman, "Drug Recovery Center CEO 'Bought' Patients With Kickbacks, Prosecutors Say," *Sun Sentinel*, August 1, 2021, https://news.yahoo.com/drug-recovery-center-ceo-bought-130800488.html?guccounter=1.

148   Freeman, "Recovery Center CEO."

149   Marc Freeman, "More Arrests to Come in Crackdown on Drug-Recovery Industry, Prosecutor Vows," *Sun Sentinel*, January 13, 2020, https://www.sun-sentinel.com/2020/01/13/more-arrests-to-come-in-crackdown-on-drug-recovery-industry-prosecutor-vows/?clearUserState=true.

150   Hanna Winston, "Jury Finds First Person Charged With Patient Brokering Not Guilty of 119 Counts," *The Palm Beach Post*, August 17, 2021, https://www.palmbeachpost.com/story/news/crime/2021/08/17/jury-finds-first-person-charged-patient-brokering-not-guilty/8149908002/.

151   *The 2022 Florida Statutes—including 2022 Special Session A and 2023 Special Session B* (leg.state.fl.us, Section 817.505(1)(a), Fla. Stat., Online Sunshine, 2022), http://www.leg.state.fl.us/Statutes/index.cfm?App_mode=Display_Statute&URL=0800-0899/0817/Sections/0817.505.html.

152   Alan Johnson, interview by Dr. Dave Campbell, May 2, 2022.

153   Chris Jacobsen, a series of interviews by Dr. Campbell in March 2020.

154   "Betty," a series of interviews by Dr. Campbell, spread over a period of three years.

155   "Health insurance rights and protections," *HealthCare.gov*, accessed. July 16, 2023, https://www.healthcare.gov/health-care-law-protections/ rate-review/.

156   John Weeks, "The 80/20 Rule: Why Medical Insurers Are Not Interested in Cost Cutting—or Integrative Health . . . plus more," *Integrative Medicine* 15, no. 5 (October 2016):18–20, https://www.ncbi.nlm.nih.gov/pmc/articles/ PMC5145008/.

157   Ted Padich, interview by Dr. Dave Campbell, July 2022.

158   Denise Corbisiero, interview by Dave Aronberg, February 9, 2021.

159   Ken Alltucker, "Arizona Lawsuit Opens Window Into Lucrative Drug Rehab Business—and Allegations of Fraud," *The Republic*, December 4, 2017, https://www.azcentral.com/story/money/business/health/2017/12/04/ arizona-lawsuit-health-net-drug-rehab-business-fraud/907734001/.

160   *Civil Court Case Information—Case History* (superiorcourt.mar- icopa.gov, The Judicial Branch of Arizona, CV2016-009984, July 22, 2017), http://www.superiorcourt.maricopa.gov/docket/CivilCourtCases/caseInfo. asp?caseNumber=CV2016-009984.

161   Alltucker, Arizona Lawsuit."

162   "Avoiding addiction treatment scams," Office of the Attorney General (MA), accessed July 17, 2023, https://www.mass.gov/service-details/ avoiding-addiction-treatment-scams

163   "Operators of South Florida Urinalysis Lab Sentenced to Prison and Ordered to Pay More than $9.6 Million in Restitution for Healthcare Fraud," U.S Department of Labor, news release, November 23, 2018, https://www.dol. gov/newsroom/releases/ebsa/ebsa20181123.

164   "The Effectiveness of Medication-Based Treatment for Opioid Use Disorder," in *Medications for Opioid Use Disorder Save Lives*, eds. Michelle Mancher and Alan I. Leshner (Washington: National Academies Press US, 2019), from Chapter 2: "Nevertheless, multiple studies with longer-term

follow-up indicate that extending treatment for years allows individuals to increase their opportunities to return to work, to regain their health, to avoid involvement with the criminal justice system, and to establish supportive networks of non-drug-using individuals."; Center for Substance Abuse Treatment, "Specialized Substance Abuse Treatment Programs," in *A Guide to Substance Abuse Services for Primary Care Clinicians*, Series, No. 24, accessed July 17, 2023, https://www.ncbi.nlm.nih.gov/books/NBK64815/.

165   Mary F. Brunette et al., "A Comparison of Long-Term and Short-Term Residential Treatment Programs for Dual Diagnosis Patients," *Psychiatric Services* 52, no. 4 (April 1, 2001), https://doi.org/10.1176/appi.ps.52.4.526.

166   Maura Dolan, "Appeals Court Backs Sober-Living Homes in Suit Against Newport Beach," *Los Angeles Times*, September 20, 2013, https://www.latimes.com/local/lanow/la-xpm-2013-sep-20-la-me-ln-newport-beach-group-homes-20130920-story.html.

167   *Fight over sober houses costly*, *South Florida Sun-Sentinel*, April 25, 2007, https://www.sun-sentinel.com/2007/04/25/fight-over-sober-houses-costly/.

168   "Best Practices for Recovery Housing," Substance Abuse and Mental Health Services Administration, 2023, https://store.samhsa.gov/sites/default/files/pep23-10-00-002.pdf.

169   U.S. Department of Housing and Urban Development and U.S. Department of Justice, "State and Local Land Use Laws and Practices and the Application of the Fair Housing Act," joint statement, November 10, 2016, https://www.justice.gov/crt/page/file/909956/download.

170   Matt Schudel. "Paul Molloy, Co-Founder of Housing Program for Addicts, Dies at 83," *Washington Post*, June 16, 2022, https://www.washingtonpost.com/obituaries/2022/06/16/paul-molloy-addiction-recovery-dies/.

171   Oxford House, "History and Accomplishments," accessed July 17, 2023, https://www.oxfordhouse.org/oxford_house_history.

172   *The 2017 Florida Statutes* (leg.state.fl.us, Online Sunshine, Chapter 397-SUBSTANCE ABUSE SERVICES Part III-CLIENT RIGHTS, ss. 397.501-307.581>397.55, Prohibition of deceptive marketing practices, accessed July 17, 2023), http://www.leg.state.fl.us/statutes/index.cfm?App_mode=Display_Statute&URL=0300-0399/0397/Sections/0397.501.html.

173   "Owner Sentenced to More than 27 Years in Prison for Multi-Million

Dollar Health Care Fraud and Money Laundering Scheme Involving Sober Homes and Alcohol and Drug Addiction Treatment Centers," U.S. Attorney's Office, Southern District of Florida, press release, May 17, 2017, https://www.justice.gov/usao-sdfl/pr/owner-sentenced-more-27-years-prison-multi-million-dollar-health-care-fraud-and-money.

174   "Florida Doctor Charged in Massive $681 Million Substance Abuse Treatment Fraud Scheme," U.S. Attorney's Office, Southern District of Florida, press release, July 31, 2020, https://www.justice.gov/usao-sdfl/pr/owner-sentenced-more-27-years-prison-multi-million-dollar-health-care-fraud-and-money.

175   Evan Wright, "The Predatory Malibu Rehab Guru Who Ripped Off Obamacare," *The Daily Beast,* May 30, 2019, https://www.thedailybeast.com/christopher-bathum-the-predatory-malibu-rehab-guru-who-ripped-off-obamacare.

176   Wright, "Predatory."

177   Wright, "Predatory."

178   Wright, "Predatory."

179   Wright, "Predatory."

180   Tony Saavedra, "So-Called 'Rehab Mogul' Raped Women, Dealt Drugs in Treatment Centers," *Orange County Register,* February 26, 2018, https://www.ocregister.com/2018/02/26/la-oc-rehab-mogul-convicted-of-sexually-exploiting-patients-and-offering-them-drugs/#:~:text=LOS%20ANGELES%20—%20A%20self%2Ddubbed,guilty%20of%2031%20criminal%20counts.

181   Nouran Salahleh, "L.A. Rehab Owner Gets More Than 52 Years in Prison for Sexually Assaulting 7 Women," *KTLA 5,* July 14, 2020, https://ktla.com/news/local-news/l-a-rehab-owner-gets-more-than-52-years-in-prison-for-sexually-assaulting-7-female-women/.

182   *Senate Bill No. 1228—An act to add Sections 11831.6 and 11831.7 to the Health and Safety Code, relating to public health* (California Legislative Information, Chapter 792, September 27, 2018), https://leginfo.legislature.ca.gov/faces/billTextClient.xhtml?bill_id=201720180SB1228.

183   Teri Sforza, "Body Brokering, Where Addicts Are Sold as Investments, Can Continue in Sober Homes, For Now," *The Orange County Register,* January 15, 2020, https://www.ocregister.com/2020/01/15/

body-brokering-where-addicts-are-sold-as-investments-can-continue-in-sober-homes-for-now/.

184   Teri Sforza, "California to Local Officials: Your Job Is to Support Sober Living Homes, Period," *The Orange County Register*, July 25, 2023, https://www.ocregister.com/2023/07/25/state-to-local-officials-your-job-is-to-support-sober-living-homes-period/.

185   Sforza, "Support."

186   Sforza, "Support."

187   "Addiction Industry Directory," National Association of Addiction Treatment Providers, accessed July 17, 2023, https://www.naatp.org/resources/addiction-industry-directory.

188   "Find a Provider," CARF International, accessed July 17, 2023, http://www.carf.org/providerSearch.aspx.

189   "Find Accredited Organizations," The Joint Commission, accessed July 17, 2023, https://www.qualitycheck.org/.

190   "NAATP Treatment Selection Guide," National Association of Addiction Treatment Providers, accessed July 17, 2023, https://www.naatp.org/resources/consumer-resources/naatp-treatment-selection-guide.

191   NAATP, "Guide."

192   *Recovery Housing: Best Practices and Suggested Guidelines* (samhsa.org, SAMHSA, accessed July 17, 2023). https://www.samhsa.gov/sites/default/files/housing-best-practices-100819.pdf

193   SAMHSA, "Key Indicators."

194   Land Development Regulation Advisory Board (LDRAB) Medical Uses Sub-Committee, meeting minutes, May 7, 201, https://discover.pbcgov.org/pzb/zoning/Hearings-Meetings-LDRABSub/MED/Agenda_05072018.pdf.

195   "Certified Providers," Florida Association of Recovery Residences (FARR), accessed July 17, 2023, http://farronline.info/providers#providers-table-pagination=1.

196   "Certification Overview," Florida Association of Recovery Residences (FARR), accessed July 17, 2023, https://farronline.org/certification/certification-overview/.

197   FARR, "Certification."

198   Seth Puja et al., "Overdose Deaths Involving Opioids, Cocaine, and Psychostimulants—United States, 2015–2016," *Morbidity and Mortality Weekly Report* 67, no. 12 (March 30, 2018): 349–358, https://pubmed.ncbi. nlm.nih.gov/29596405/.

ABOUT THE AUTHORS

DAVE ARONBERG recently completed three terms as state attorney for Palm Beach County. He is a former state senator, Florida assistant attorney general and White House Fellow in the U.S. Department of the Treasury. A graduate of Harvard College and Harvard Law School, he is currently a guest legal analyst on MSNBC, CNN and NewsNation.

DAVID R. CAMPBELL, MD, FAAOS, is an orthopedic surgeon practicing in Florida and was an assistant professor of orthopedic surgery in the College of Medicine at the University of Central Florida. He is a retired major in the United States Army Reserve Medical Corps and author of The Teen Formula: A Parent's Guide to Helping Your Child Avoid Substance Abuse. A graduate of Columbia College and the University of Miami School of Medicine, he has been the chief medical correspondent for MSNBC's Morning Joe and a medical contributor for MSNBC and NBC.

www.ingramcontent.com/pod-product-compliance
Lightning Source LLC
Chambersburg PA
CBHW062217270326
41930CB00009B/1761